An Anglican Prayer Book

Published for
The Anglican Mission in the Americas
P.O. Box 3427
Pawleys Island, SC 29585
www.theamia.org
by
Preservation Press of the Prayer Book Society of the U.S.A.
P.O. Box 35220
Philadelphia, PA 19128-0220
www.pbsusa.org

2008

ISBN: 978-1-879793-13-2 and 1-879793-13-X

Designed and Typeset by Boldface Graphics, Houston
www.boldfacegraphics.com

Printed in the U.S.A.

An Anglican Prayer Book

Contemporary English Services
based on those in
The Book of Common Prayer and
The Ordinal,
in their English 1662,
American 1928, and
Canadian 1962
editions

Preservation Press of the Prayer Book Society of the U.S.A.
2008

Contents

Preface vii
The Christian Year x
Morning and Evening Prayer 1
The Litany 25
The Athanasian Creed or Quicunque Vult 34
An Order for Compline 37
The Order for the Holy Communion 43
The Collects and Eucharistic Lectionary 75
Baptism 111
The Catechism 121
Confirmation 132
The Solemnization of Holy Matrimony 138
Visitation of the Sick 149
The Burial of the Dead 155
Interment or Scattering of Ashes 163
Daily Prayer for Use in Families 165
The Daily Lectionary 172
The Ordinal 185
The Form and Manner of Making of Deacons 187
The Form and Manner of Ordaining of Priests 192
The Form of Ordaining or Consecrating of a Bishop 202
The Thirty-Nine Articles of Religion 210
Acknowledgements 227

Preface

It is our joy and privilege to commend *An Anglican Prayer Book* (2008) as a part of the renewing of The Anglican Way in North America. Though it is in contemporary English and in modern format, it belongs to a long and rich tradition and pedigree of worship and doctrine, especially that contained in the English Prayer Book, which itself looks back to the patristic and biblical roots of Christian worship.

The Book of Common Prayer (1662) is not only the primary Prayer Book of the Church of England, but also of many other Anglican Churches as well. It has been translated into over one hundred and fifty languages. In the United States of America, *The Book of Common Prayer* (1928) is based upon it, as is also *The Book of Common Prayer* (1962) of Canada. Together with *The Thirty-Nine Articles* and *The Form and Manner of Making, Ordaining and Consecrating of Bishops, Priests and Deacons* (The Ordinal), it is regarded as a Formulary, that is, a standard of doctrine of The Anglican Way. This has been recognized continually by the Lambeth Conference of Anglican Bishops for the last century and more.

The Book of Common Prayer (1662) had its origins in *The Booke of the Common Prayer* (1549), which was created from the multiple service books of the medieval English Church by Archbishop Thomas Cranmer and others. In its editions of 1552, 1559, 1604, and then 1662, it contained the worship, doctrine and discipline that is now referred to as Reformed Catholicism or The Anglican Way.

The original language of this traditional Prayer Book is a particular religious form of the English language as it was developing in the sixteenth century; and it was given its polished and memorable form by the literary genius of Archbishop Cranmer. At the heart of it is the use of the second person singular (thou/thee/thy/thine) for God to emphasize both his unity, and the

Preface

intimacy of communion with him by his adopted children. It also has a style and rhythm, which make it both pleasant to read and hear, and easy to remember. Its natural companion is the King James Version of the Bible (1611), known in England as The Authorized Version.

In the twenty-first century, a majority of English-speaking Christians desire to address God in a dignified form of the language commonly used today. The danger is, however, for Anglicans that, in creating new liturgy using contemporary English, the biblical and classic doctrine of Reformed Catholicism can so easily be neglected or denied. Therefore, it was resolved to render the substance of *The Book of Common Prayer* (1662; with its 1928 & 1962 editions) into a dignified form of contemporary English, in which God is addressed as "You," and without losing the classical heritage of doctrine and devotion.

As so much of this Prayer Book is from or related to the Bible, a choice had to be made as to which modern version was to be recommended for the public reading of the Scriptures, as set out in the Lectionary. The English Standard Version was chosen because it is in the tradition of the King James Version, and is an updated form of the Revised Standard Version (which is also recommended), without the modern "inclusivism" of the New Revised Standard Version and other popular versions.

There is neither a simple nor single way of rendering classic texts written in the historic English language of prayer into contemporary English, even as there is not one form of contemporary English. There is not yet a contemporary English language of prayer. What is presented in this collection of services is a conservative rendering in both style and doctrine. It has been a major concern in preparing it to retain the basic teaching within the Prayer Book of 1662, and to do so in as dignified style and form as possible.

For a congregation to use this book profitably, its clergy and lay leaders will also need to be familiar with *The Book of Common Prayer* (editions of 1662; 1928 & 1962), in order to obtain a working knowledge of the original text and how it was intended for use

Preface

in public worship. Having this information will make it easier to use the present contemporary version profitably. And, of course, it is the original that remains the Formulary and thus possesses authority as the standard of doctrine.

The rubrics or instructions in the original text (usually provided in italics) have only been followed in general terms in this contemporary version. This is to take account of both greater congregational participation and more flexibility in the use of spiritual songs and hymns. It is presumed that Bishops will provide guidelines concerning such participation and flexibility. In terms of the singing of Canticles and Psalms, the publication of this Prayer Book provides an incentive for musicians to compose appropriate, new music for use in public worship.

The work of preparing this contemporary version of *An Anglican Prayer Book* has been done in the first place for the Anglican Mission in the Americas, which is a missionary arm and a part of the African Anglican Province of Rwanda. The Rev'd Dr. Peter Toon, President of The Prayer Book Society of the U.S.A., has been primarily responsible for guiding this work to completion. It is expected that the Services in this Book will also be used by other Anglicans and Episcopalians both in North America and elsewhere in the English-speaking world.

We hope that *An Anglican Prayer Book* will help to advance the Gospel of Jesus within the Church and to the world in the twenty-first century; and we pray that it will do so by encouraging holy worship both "in spirit and in truth" and the "beauty of holiness," together with outreach and mission, that are biblically-based and within the rich tradition of the Anglican Way.

The Right Rev'd Charles Hurt Murphy III
The Right Rev'd John Rodgers Jr.
Anglican Mission in the Americas.
www.theamia.org
January 2008

The Christian Year

The Church's Calendar is planned to remind the Christian people of the great events of the Gospel story, out of which Christian worship springs. Thus *Sunday* is the weekly memorial of the Resurrection of our Lord Jesus Christ; and, at the same time, it partakes of the Season in which it occurs.

For every Sunday, and the chief commemorations in the year, a Collect, Epistle and Gospel are provided (with an O.T. Reading and Psalm also for Holy Communion where it does not immediately follow Morning Prayer). The Collect often sets the note of the day's worship. The Gospels are from the Gospel story and the Epistles usually from the pastoral messages of Apostles to their people.

The Psalms are read through in daily portions at Morning and Evening Prayer, but special Psalms are selected for Sundays and for the chief festivals. The Lectionary provides for the orderly reading of the Bible morning and evening throughout the year, with special lessons for Sundays.

The sequence of the Church's year is as follows:

Advent prepares us to celebrate the first coming of Jesus Christ, and warns us that he will come again to judge the living and the dead.

Christmas, the anniversary of our Lord's birth on December 25, leads to *Epiphany* on January 6, which, with the following Sundays, speaks of the glory of God revealed in Jesus Christ.

Septuagesima, Sexagesima, and *Quinquagesima,* so-called because they precede Easter by approximately seventy, sixty, and fifty days, bridge the interval between the Epiphany season and

Lent, which begins on Ash Wednesday, and lasts, excluding Sundays, for forty days, recalling the forty days of our Lord's temptation in the wilderness. It is a season of penitence and fasting in preparation for Easter. The fifth Sunday in Lent, called Passion Sunday, foreshadows

The Christian Year

Holy Week which, opening on Palm Sunday, leads our thoughts through our Lord's Passion, from his entry into Jerusalem, through the Last Supper on Maundy Thursday, to his Crucifixion on Good Friday, and his lying in the grave on Easter Eve.

Easter, the festival of the Resurrection, is kept for eight days, the "octave." Its date varies according to the date of the Passover full moon. The season of rejoicing extends through the forty days to

Ascension Day, when Christ ascends and is proclaimed the Lord of all life; and then ten days later to

Whitsunday, also called Pentecost, when the Holy Spirit came to dwell in the Church. The series ends with

Trinity Sunday, which declares the fullness of the Christian revelation of God as Three Persons, One Godhead. The following Sundays to Advent are named "after Trinity."

Holy Days and Saints' Days. Other events in our Lord's life are also commemorated during the year. Saints are remembered on special days; and on November 1, All Saints' Day, the list closes with the vision of the Church triumphant.

Morning and Evening Prayer

Introduction

The discipline and practice of Morning and Evening Prayer not only fit into a basic rhythm of nature, but were also what occurred publicly in the Early Church before the development of monasticism and the multiplication of daily services within this movement. In the sixteenth century, at the Protestant Reformation, the Church of England abandoned the medieval monastic model of many daily services. It returned to the discipline of two services daily, making these available for all Christians, clergy and laity alike, and requiring the clergy to use them in church, after ringing the bell to notify parishioners.

The content of both Morning and Evening Prayer is primarily portions of the Christian Bible. There are readings from the Old and New Testaments, the praying of Psalms from the Psalter, the use of Canticles usually taken from the Bible or Apocrypha, and the offering of prayers, whose very language is often a medley of Biblical phrases. Of course, all this occurs within a structure, which is intended to make the praise of the Lord, and the offering of prayer to him, follow a path that is in accord with the godly experience of the centuries, in terms of relating to God in a humble, penitent manner.

In order to offer Morning & Evening Prayer to the Father through the Son and with the Holy Spirit in an orderly and reverent way, the Minister and people require not only the text of the Services, but also a Bible, the Collects for the Christian Year, and a Lectionary (Table of Daily Readings and Psalms). The two latter are provided below. The version of the Bible recommended for use in Daily Prayer is the English Standard Version; but other versions such as the RSV and the NKJV can be used.

The Daily Services can begin at one of two points. The first is at the beginning where the reading of Scripture sentences is a call to prepare for worshipping the Lord in spirit and in truth. When Morning or Evening Prayer is a primary service of the day then obviously this is the place to begin, so that the whole scope

Morning and Evening Prayer

of the content is used to full effect for the encounter with God. However, if the Service is to be followed by either The Litany or by The Order for Holy Communion, or used in the home, then it can begin at the prayer, "Open our lips, O Lord."

In its full form the daily Service may be said to have four parts, which overlap a little. (1) The Penitential Introduction, ending with the Absolution; (2) The Service of Praise and Thanksgiving; (3) The Reading of the Holy Scriptures and the Profession of Faith, and (4) The Prayers and Thanksgivings.

If the Service is to be sung in whole or part, then there will be need locally both to adapt the preferred music to the words and/or to adapt the words to the music. There is, of course, also opportunity to compose new music, which glorifies God.

The use of the Athanasian Creed (known also by its original, opening Latin words, Quicunque vult) is most useful and helpful in making clear what the Church believes and teaches concerning God, the Holy Trinity, and the full identity of Jesus of Nazareth. It is, therefore, most appropriate that it be used not only on Trinity Sunday but also on other occasions also as a substitute for The Apostles' Creed.

The traditional use of the Litany is after Morning Prayer on Wednesday and Friday, and after Morning Prayer and before Holy Communion on some Sundays; but it may be used at other times as well.

Since the structure of Morning and Evening Prayer is virtually identical, the two are printed here as one Service, but with the traditional Canticles and Collects for each clearly indicated.

When either Morning or Evening Prayer is a main service of the Lord's Day, a sermon is preached at the end of the Office. Further, public Baptism may be performed within this Office, as indicated in the instructions for that Service.

For those whose circumstances make saying Evening Prayer difficult or impossible, or who wish a late evening Office, the ancient, short Office of Compline is provided after the Daily Office below.

Morning and Evening Prayer

The Service of Morning and Evening Prayer

The Service may begin with the singing of a hymn, the people standing.

The Minister reads one or more of the following Sentences of Scripture, the people standing and remaining so until the Confession.

For any occasion

THE Lord is in his holy temple, let all the earth keep silence before him. *Hab. 2:20*

I was glad when they said to me, "Let us go to the house of the Lord!" *Psalm 122:1*

Let the words of my mouth and the meditation of my heart be acceptable in your sight, Lord, my rock and my redeemer. *Psalm 19:4*

Send out your light and your truth; let them lead me; let them bring me to your holy hill and to your dwelling! *Psalm 43:3*

For thus says the One who is high and lifted up, who inhabits eternity, whose name is Holy. "I dwell in the high and holy place, and also with him who is of a contrite and lowly spirit, to revive the spirit of the lowly, and to revive the heart of the contrite." *Isaiah 57:15*

The hour is coming, and is now here, when the true worshippers will worship the Father in spirit and in truth, for the Father is seeking such people to worship him. *John 4:23*

Morning and Evening Prayer

Grace to you and peace from God our Father and from the Lord Jesus Christ. *Phil.1:2*

If we confess our sins, God is faithful and just to forgive us our sins and to cleanse us from all unrighteousness. *1 John 1:9*

Advent

Repent for the kingdom of heaven is at hand. *Matt. 3:2*

In the wilderness prepare the way of the Lord; make straight in the desert a highway for our God. *Isaiah 40:3*

Christmas

Fear not, for behold, I bring you good news of a great joy that will be for all the people. For unto you is born this day in the city of David a Savior, who is Christ the Lord. *Luke 2:10,11*

In this was the love of God made manifest among us, that God sent his only Son into the world, so that we might live through him. *1 John 4:9*

Epiphany

From the rising of the sun to its setting God's name will be great among the nations, and in every place incense will be offered to his name, and a pure offering. For my name will be great among the nations, says the Lord of hosts. *Mal. 1:11*

Awake, awake, put on your strength, Zion; put on your beautiful garments, Jerusalem. *Isaiah 52:1*

Morning and Evening Prayer

Lent

Tear your hearts and not your garments. Return to the Lord, your God, for he is gracious and merciful, slow to anger, and abounding in steadfast love; and he relents over disaster. *Joel 2:13*

The sacrifices of God are a broken spirit; and a broken and a contrite heart he will not despise. *Psalm 51:17*

I will arise and go to my father, and will say to him, "Father, I have sinned against heaven and before you. I am no longer worthy to be called your son." *Luke 15: 18,19*

Good Friday

Is it nothing to you, all you who pass by? Look and see if there is any sorrow like my sorrow, which was brought upon me, which the Lord inflicted. *Lam. 1:12*

In Christ Jesus we have redemption through his blood, the forgiveness of our sins, according to the riches of his grace. *Eph.1:7*

Easter

Christ Jesus is risen from the dead. The Lord has risen indeed. *Luke 24:34*

This is the day that the Lord has made; let us rejoice and be glad it in. *Psalm 118:24*

Ascension

Since we have a great high priest, who has passed through the heavens, Jesus, the Son of God, let us then with confidence draw near to the throne of grace, that

Morning and Evening Prayer

we may receive mercy and find grace to help in time of need. *Heb. 4:14,16*

Whitsuntide/ Pentecost

You will receive power when the Holy Spirit has come upon you, and you will be my witnesses in Jerusalem and in all Judea and Samaria, and to the ends of the earth. *Acts 1:8*

Because you are sons, God has sent the Spirit of his Son into your hearts, crying, "Abba, Father!" *Gal. 4:6*

Trinity Sunday

"Holy, holy, holy, is the Lord God Almighty, who was and is and is to come." *Rev.4:8*

All Saints' Day

Since we are surrounded by so great a cloud of witnesses, let us lay aside every weight, and sin which clings closely, and let us run with endurance the race that is set before us looking unto Jesus the founder and perfecter of our faith. *Heb. 12:1–2*

Then the Minister says,

BROTHERS and Sisters, the Holy Scripture calls us, in various places, to acknowledge and confess our many sins and wickedness; and that we should not try to hide them before the face of Almighty God our heavenly Father; but confess them with a humble, lowly, penitent and obedient heart; so that we may obtain forgiveness of them by his infinite goodness and

Morning and Evening Prayer

mercy. And although we ought, at all times, humbly to acknowledge our sins before God; we ought to do so especially when we assemble and come together to give thanks for the great blessings that we have received at his hands, to offer the praise that is due to him, to hear his most holy Word, and to ask him to supply our needs of body and soul. So I invite you to approach the throne of heavenly grace with me, humbly and with pure intent, saying,

Or he says,

Let us humbly confess our sins to Almighty God.

A General Confession is said by the whole Congregation together with the Minister, all keeling.

ALMIGHTY and most merciful Father, we have erred and strayed from your ways like lost sheep. We have followed too much the evil intentions and desires of our own hearts. We have broken your holy laws. We have left undone the things that we ought to have done; and we have done the things that we ought not to have done; and there is no spiritual soundness within us. Have mercy on us, pitiful sinners, O Lord. Spare those who confess their sins. Restore those who truly repent, even as you have promised through Jesus Christ our Lord. And grant, merciful Father, for his sake, that we may live from this time forward a godly, righteous and holy life, to the glory of your holy Name. Amen.

Morning and Evening Prayer

> The Declaration of Absolution, or Forgiveness of sins, is to be made by the Priest alone, standing, as the People continue to kneel. The Priest, at his discretion, may use, instead of what follows, the Absolution from the Service of Holy Communion.

ALMIGHTY God, the Father of our Lord Jesus Christ, does not desire the death of sinners, but rather that they may turn from their wickedness and live. He has commanded and authorized his Ministers to assure his people that they will receive absolution and forgiveness when they repent of their sins. God, the Father, pardons and forgives all who truly repent and sincerely believe his holy gospel. Therefore, let us ask him to grant us true repentance and his Holy Spirit; so that what we do now may please him, that the rest of our lives may be pure and holy, and that finally we may come to his eternal joy; through Jesus Christ our Lord. *Amen.*

> Instead of the above, in the absence of a priest, a deacon or lay person may pray on behalf of all,

MERCIFUL God, grant to your faithful people pardon and peace; that they may be cleansed from all their sins, and serve you with a quiet mind; through Jesus Christ our Lord. *Amen.*

> Then the Minister kneels, and with the people says the Lord's Prayer either in the traditional or contemporary form.

Morning and Evening Prayer

Traditional

Our Father who art in heaven, Hallowed be thy Name, Thy kingdom come, Thy will be done, on earth as it is in heaven. Give us this day our daily bread; And forgive us our trespasses, as we forgive them that trespass against us; And lead us not into temptation, but deliver us from evil. For thine is the kingdom, the power and the glory, forever and ever. Amen.

Contemporary

Our Father in heaven, hallowed be your name. Your kingdom come, your will be done, on earth as in heaven. Give us today our daily bread. Forgive us our sins as we forgive those who sin against us. Lead us not into temptation but deliver us from evil. For yours is the kingdom, and the power, and the glory, forever and ever. Amen.

Minister: Open our lips, O Lord.
People: And we shall declare your praise.
Minister: O God, make speed to save us.
People: O Lord, make haste to help us.

All stand.

Minister: Glory be to the Father and to the Son and to the Holy Spirit:
People: As it was in the beginning, is now, and shall be forever; world without end. Amen.
Minister: Let us praise the Lord.
People: The Lord's Name be praised.

Morning and Evening Prayer

Here the appointed Psalm(s) is said or sung, which at Morning Prayer may include daily, Psalm 95, as the first. At the end of each Psalm the Gloria Patri is used: **Glory be to the Father, and to the Son, and to the Holy Spirit: As it was in the beginning, is now, and shall be forever; world without end. Amen.**

The congregation sits. Then the Old Testament Lesson is read, introduced as follows: **Here begins the _ verse of the _ chapter of the Book of _ .** After it is completed, the Reader says: **Here ends the first Lesson.**

The congregation stands. Then is said or sung a Canticle, normally **Te Deum Laudamus** at Morning Prayer, and **Magnificat (Luke 1:46)** at Evening Prayer. For alternatives see the Appendix to the Service. At the discretion of the Minister, the final section of **Te Deum** may be omitted.

Te Deum—Morning Prayer

WE praise you, O God; we acknowledge you to be the Lord.

All creation worships you; the everlasting Father.

To you all the angels and the powers of heaven loudly cry,

To you cherubim and seraphim continually sing,

Holy, holy, holy, Lord God of hosts;

Heaven and earth are full of the majesty of your glory.

THE glorious company of the apostles praise you:

The noble fellowship of the prophets praise you.

The white-robed army of martyrs praise you.

Morning and Evening Prayer

The holy Church throughout all the world acclaims you;
The Father, of majesty unbounded;
Your adorable, true and only Son;
And the Holy Spirit, the Counselor.

You are the King of glory, Lord Christ.
 You are the everlasting Son of the Father.
When you became man to set us free, you humbled yourself to be born of a Virgin.
When you had overcome the sting of death, you opened the kingdom of heaven to all believers.
You sit at the right hand of God, in the glory of the Father.
We believe that you will come again to be our Judge.
Come then, Lord, we pray, and help your servants, whom you have redeemed with your precious blood.
Bring us to be united with your saints, in everlasting glory.

O Lord, save your people, and bless your inheritance.
Govern them, and uphold them now and always.
Day by day we glorify you;
And we worship your Name always, forever and ever.
O Lord, by your grace, keep us this day from all sin.
O Lord, have mercy on us, have mercy on us.

Morning and Evening Prayer

O Lord, let your mercy rest upon us, for we put our trust in you.

O Lord, I have trusted in you; let me not be abandoned at the last.

Magnificat—Evening Prayer

My soul magnifies the Lord, and my spirit rejoices in God my Savior;

For he has looked on the humble state of his servant;

For behold from now on all generations will call me blessed;

For he who is mighty has done great things for me, and holy is his name;

And his mercy is for those who fear him, from generation to generation.

He has shown strength with his arm, he has scattered the proud in the thoughts of their hearts;

He has brought down the mighty from their thrones, and exalted those of humble state;

He has filled the hungry with good things, and the rich he has sent empty away;

He has helped his servant Israel, in remembrance of his mercy;

As he spoke to our fathers, to Abraham and to his offspring forever.

Glory be to the Father, and to the Son, and to the Holy Spirit:

As it was in the beginning, is now, and shall be forever; world without end. Amen.

Morning and Evening Prayer

The congregation sits. Then the New Testament lesson is read, introduced and ended in the same way as the Old Testament lesson.

The congregation stands to say or sing **Benedictus Dominus (Luke 1:68)** at Morning and **Nunc Dimittis (Luke 2:29)** at Evening Prayer.

Benedictus—Morning Prayer

Blessed be the Lord God of Israel, for he has visited and redeemed his people;

And has raised up a horn of salvation for us, in the house of his servant David;

As he spoke by the mouth of his holy prophets, from of old;

That we should be saved from our enemies, and from the hand of all who hate us;

To show the mercy promised to our forebears, and to remember his holy covenant;

The oath that he swore to our father Abraham, to grant us;

That we, being delivered from the hand of our enemies, might serve him without fear;

In holiness and righteousness before him, all our days;

And you, child, will be called the prophet of the Most High, for you will go before the Lord to prepare his ways;

To give knowledge of salvation to his people, in the forgiveness of their sins;

Because of the tender mercy of our God, whereby the sunrise shall visit us from on high;

Morning and Evening Prayer

To give light to those who sit in darkness and in the shadow of death, to guide our feet into the way of peace.

Glory be to the Father, and to the Son, and to the Holy Spirit:

As it was in the beginning, is now, and shall be forever; world without end. Amen.

Nunc Dimittis—Evening Prayer

LORD, now you are letting your servant depart in peace, according to your word;

For my eyes have seen your salvation, that you have prepared in the sight of all peoples;

A light for revelation to the Gentiles, and for glory to your people Israel.

Glory be to the Father, and to the Son, and to the Holy Spirit:

As it was in the beginning, is now, and shall be forever; world without end. Amen

All remain standing to say the Apostles' Creed (or The Athanasian Creed).

I BELIEVE in God the Father Almighty, creator of heaven and earth. And I believe in Jesus Christ, his only Son, our Lord. He was conceived by the Holy Spirit and born of the Virgin Mary. He suffered under Pontius Pilate, was crucified, died and was buried. He descended to the dead[or into hell]. On the third day he rose again. He ascended into heaven and sits at the right hand of God the Father Almighty. From there he shall come

Morning and Evening Prayer

to judge the living and the dead. I believe in the Holy Spirit; the holy Catholic Church; the communion of saints; the forgiveness of sins; the resurrection of the body, and the life everlasting. Amen.

Minister: The Lord be with you.
People: And with your spirit.
Minister: Let us pray.

> The congregation kneels. Here follows the Lord's Prayer if it has not already been said.

Minister: O Lord, show us your mercy.
People: And grant us your salvation.
Minister: Endue your Ministers with righteousness.
People: And make your chosen people joyful.
Minister: O Lord, save your people.
People: And bless your inheritance.
Minister: Give peace in our time, Lord.
People: For you alone rule the world.
Minister: Cleanse our hearts, O Lord.
People: And revive us by your Holy Spirit.

> The Collect for the Day follows, except when the Communion Service is to follow; and then the Collect for the Day is omitted here.

At **Morning Prayer** these two Collects are said.

The Second Collect, for Peace

LORD God, the author of peace and lover of harmony, whom to know is eternal life and to serve is perfect freedom: defend us your humble servants against all

Morning and Evening Prayer

assaults of our enemies, that trusting in your defense, we may not fear the power of any adversaries; through the might of Jesus Christ our Lord. *Amen.*

The Third Collect, for Grace

Heavenly Father, Almighty and Everlasting God, we thank you that you have brought us safely to the beginning of this day; defend us, your humble servants, with your mighty power, and grant that we neither fall into sin, nor run into any kind of danger; also grant that, being guided and governed by you, we may do what is right in your sight; through Jesus Christ our Lord. *Amen.*

At **Evening Prayer** these two Collects are said.

The Second Collect, for Peace

Lord God, the author of all holy desires, all good purposes, and all righteous works; give to us your servants that peace which the world cannot give; so that we, obeying your commandments and being delivered from the fear of our enemies, may live at rest and in quietness; through the merits of Jesus Christ our Savior. *Amen.*

The Third Collect, for Aid against all Perils.

Lighten our darkness, Lord, we pray, and by your great mercy defend us from all perils and dangers of this night; for the love of your only Son, our Savior Jesus Christ. *Amen.*

The fixed Order ends here.

Morning and Evening Prayer

Here a Hymn or Anthem may be sung and then be followed by a Sermon and/or by the use of the Prayers printed below; or by a time of silent prayer with biddings; or by The Litany; or by other forms of guided intercession. The Service ends with A Prayer of Saint Chrysostom and The Grace.

A Prayer for all in Civil Authority.

LORD God, our Governor, whose glory is in all the world; we commend this nation to your merciful care, that being guided by your providence, we may dwell secure in your peace. Grant to [*here the appropriate persons in government are named*] and to all in authority, wisdom and strength to know and to do your will. Fill them with the love of truth and righteousness; and make them always mindful of their calling to serve this nation and people in reverence before you; through Jesus Christ our Lord, who lives and reigns with you and the Holy Spirit, one God, now and forever. *Amen*.

A Prayer for the Clergy and People.

ALMIGHTY and everlasting God, from whom comes every good and perfect gift: send down upon our Bishops and other Clergy, and on the congregations which they serve, your life-giving Spirit of grace; and, that they may truly please you, pour upon them the continuing refreshment of your blessing. Grant this, we pray, for the honor of our Advocate and Mediator, Jesus Christ. *Amen*.

A Prayer for all People.

O GOD, the Creator and Preserver of all the world, we humbly pray that you will reveal your ways to

Morning and Evening Prayer

people of every kind and type, and your saving power to all nations. In particular, we pray for your holy, catholic Church that it may be guided and governed by your good Spirit, that all who profess and call themselves Christians may be led into the way of truth and hold the faith in unity of spirit, in the bond of peace, and in righteousness of life. Finally, we commend to your fatherly goodness all those who are in any way afflicted, or distressed, in mind, body, personal welfare or material circumstances [*especially those for whom our prayers are desired*]. Be pleased, holy Father, to comfort and relieve them according to their various needs; give them patience under their suffering, and a happy deliverance out of their afflictions; for Jesus Christ's sake. *Amen.*

A Prayer for God's continual help.

Go before us, Lord, in all our doings, with your most gracious favor, and further us with your continual help; that in all our works begun, continued and ended in you, we may glorify your holy name, and finally by your mercy attain everlasting life; through Jesus Christ our Lord. *Amen.*

A General Thanksgiving.

ALMIGHTY God, Father of all mercies, we your unworthy servants give you most humble and sincere thanks for all your goodness and loving-kindness to us and to all people; We bless you for our creation, preservation, and all the blessings of this life; but, above all,

Morning and Evening Prayer

for your immeasurable love in the redemption of the world by our Lord Jesus Christ, for the means of grace and for the hope of glory. Give us, we pray, such a sense of all your mercies that our hearts may be sincerely thankful, so that we declare your praise not only with our lips, but also in our lives, by giving up ourselves to your service, and by walking before you in holiness and righteousness all our days; through Jesus Christ our Lord, to whom, with you and the Holy Spirit, be all honor and glory, forever and ever. *Amen.*

A Prayer of Saint Chrysostom.

ALMIGHTY God, you who have given us grace at this time to bring before you with one mind our common petitions, and have promised that when two or three are gathered together in your Name you will grant their requests: we humbly ask you to fulfill now the desires and petitions of your servants, in ways that are most suitable for them, granting us in this world knowledge of your truth, and in the world to come everlasting life; through Jesus Christ our Lord. *Amen.*

The Grace, 2 Corinthians 13:14.

THE grace of our Lord Jesus Christ, and the love of God, and the fellowship of the Holy Spirit, be with us all evermore. *Amen.*

Appendix—Canticles

The usual Canticles for Morning Prayer are *Venite* (Psalm 95) before the appointed Psalm[s]); *Te Deum*, or *Benedictus Es*, or *Benedicite*, after the O.T. Lesson, and *Benedictus* (Luke 1:68–79), or

Morning and Evening Prayer

Jubilate Deo (Psalm 100) after the N.T. Lesson.

The usual Canticles for Evening Prayer are *Magnificat* (Luke 1:46–53) or *Cantate Domino* (Psalm 98) after the O.T. Lesson, and *Nunc Dimittis* (Luke 2:29–32) or *Deus Misereatur* (Psalm 67) after the N.T. Lesson. *Phos Hilaron* may be used before the Psalter on occasion, especially on the Eve of Feast Days.

Below are Canticles which are from the Apocrypha (Greek Book of Daniel) or productions of the Early Church (e.g., *Phos Hilaron*). Also The Easter and Whitsuntide Anthems, which are a medley of Bible verses, are also provided. These can be used during Easter and Whitsuntide and on other occasions, as required.

Benedictus es, Domine (from *The Song of the Three Young Men* in the Apocrypha)

BLESSED are you, Lord, the God of our fathers: worthy of praise, and highly exalted forever.

Blessed is your holy and glorious Name: to be highly praised and highly exalted forever.

Blessed are you in your holy and glorious temple: most worthy to be hymned and glorified forever.

Blessed are you seated between the cherubim and beholding the depths: worthy of praise and highly exalted forever.

Blessed are you on your royal throne: worthy of praise and highly exalted forever.

Blessed are you in the dome of heaven: worthy to be hymned and glorified forever.

Let us bless the Father, the Son and the Holy Spirit: sing praise to him and highly exalt him forever.

Morning and Evening Prayer

Benedicite, omnia opera Domini (from *The Song of the Three Young Men* in the Apocrypha)

Let the whole creation bless the Lord: sing his praise and exalt him forever.

Bless the Lord, you heavens: sing his praise and exalt him forever.

Bless the Lord, you angels of the Lord: sing his praise and exalt him forever.

Bless the Lord, all you waters above the heavens: sing his praise and exalt him forever.

Bless the Lord, all you his hosts: sing his praise and exalt him forever.

Bless the Lord, sun and moon: sing his praise and exalt him forever.

Bless the Lord, stars of heaven: sing his praise and exalt him forever.

Bless the Lord, all rain and dew: sing his praise and exalt him forever.

Bless the Lord, all winds that blow: sing his praise and exalt him forever.

Bless the Lord, fire and heat: sing his praise and exalt him forever.

Bless the Lord, scorching blast and bitter cold: sing his praise and exalt him forever.

Bless the Lord, dews and falling snow: sing his praise and exalt him forever.

Bless the Lord, nights and days: sing his praise and exalt him forever.

Morning and Evening Prayer

Bless the Lord, light and darkness: sing his praise and exalt him forever.

Bless the Lord, frosts and cold: sing his praise and exalt him forever.

Bless the Lord, ice and snow: sing his praise and exalt him forever.

Bless the Lord, lightnings and clouds: sing his praise and exalt him forever.

Let the earth bless the Lord: sing his praise and exalt him forever.

Bless the Lord, mountains and hills: sing his praise and exalt him forever.

Bless the Lord, all that grows in the earth: sing his praise and exalt him forever.

Bless the Lord, springs and wells: sing his praise and exalt him forever.

Bless the Lord, seas and rivers: sing his praise and exalt him forever.

Bless the Lord, you whales and all creatures that move in the waters: sing his praise and exalt him forever.

Bless the Lord, all birds of the air: sing his praise and exalt him forever.

Bless the Lord, all beasts and cattle: sing his praise and exalt him forever.

Bless the Lord, all people on earth: sing his praise and exalt him forever.

Bless the Lord, O Israel: sing his praise and exalt him forever.

Morning and Evening Prayer

Bless the Lord, you priests of the Lord: sing his praise and exalt him forever.

Bless the Lord, you servants of the Lord: sing his praise and exalt him forever.

Bless the Lord, spirits and souls of the righteous: sing his praise and exalt him forever.

Bless the Lord, you who are holy and humble in heart: sing his praise and exalt him forever.

Let us bless the Father, and the Son, and the Holy Spirit: sing praise to him and highly exalt him forever.

Phos hilaron—a Song of the Light

JOYFUL light,
From the pure glory of the eternal heavenly Father,
O holy, blessed Jesus Christ.
As we come to the setting of the sun
And see the evening light,
We give thanks and praise to the Father and to the Son
And to the Holy Spirit of God.
Worthy are you at all times
To be praised with holy voices,
Son of God, Giver of life,
And to be glorified through all creation.

The Easter Anthems—2 Corinthians 5:7–8; Romans 6:9–11; 1 Corinthians 15:20–22

CHRIST our Passover has been sacrificed for us: therefore let us celebrate the feast. Not with the old leaven of corruption and wickedness; but with the unleavened bread of sincerity and truth.

Morning and Evening Prayer

Christ, once raised from the dead dies no more; death has no more dominion over him.

In dying, he died to sin once for all; in living, he lives to God. See yourselves therefore as dead to sin: and alive to God in Jesus Christ our Lord.

Christ has been raised from the dead: the first-fruits of those who sleep. For as by man came death: by man has come also the resurrection of the dead. For as in Adam all die: even so in Christ shall all be made alive.

Glory be to the Father, and to the Son, and to the Holy Spirit: as it was in the beginning, is now, and shall be forever; world without end. Amen.

The Whitsuntide Anthems—Psalm 98:1; Acts 2:33; Galatians 4:6; 2 Corinthians 3:18

Sing to the Lord a new song, for he has done marvelous things.

Being therefore exalted at the right hand of God, and having received from the Father the promise of the Holy Spirit, he has poured out this that you yourselves are seeing and hearing.

And because you are sons, God has sent the Spirit of his Son into our hearts, crying, "Abba, Father."

We all, with unveiled face, beholding the glory of the Lord, are being transformed into the same image from one degree of glory to another.

Glory be to the Father and to the Son and to the Holy Spirit: as it was in the beginning, is now, and shall be forever; world without end. Amen.

The Litany
Introduction

A litany is a particular form of prayer in which there is a dynamic, spiritual movement between the Minister and the congregation. The Minister calls upon the people to pray for this and that (biddings), calls upon the Lord (invocations), and makes requests (petitions); and, in all three instances, there is a response from the people.

The original English Litany, upon which that in the Prayer Book is based, was published, with the music, in 1544, some five years before the appearance of the first edition of The Book of Common Prayer. In the Anglican tradition, the use of the Litany has been particularly associated with Wednesdays and Fridays, following Morning Prayer; before Holy Communion on certain Sundays and Holy Days, and at ordinations of deacons, priests and bishops. It can be sung or said. It is also easily adapted for use at a midweek prayer meeting in church before the offering of ex tempore prayers, and, from time to time, as part of family prayer.

The Minister says or sings the petitions, and the people join in the responses. Some of the petitions in each section may be omitted. The Litany may also be sung in procession.

GOD the Father, Creator of heaven and earth: have mercy on us.

God the Father, Creator of heaven and earth: have mercy on us.

God the Son, Redeemer of the world: have mercy on us.

God the Son, Redeemer of the world: have mercy on us.

The Litany

God the Holy Spirit, Sanctifier of the faithful: have mercy on us.
God the Holy Spirit, Sanctifier of the faithful: have mercy on us.

Holy, blessed, and glorious Trinity, three Persons and one God: have mercy on us.
Holy, blessed, and glorious Trinity, three Persons and one God: have mercy on us.

Do not remember, Lord Christ, our sins or the sins of our parents, and do not take vengeance for our offenses. Spare us, good Lord; spare your people, whom you have redeemed with your precious blood, and do not be angry with us forever.
Spare us, good Lord.

From all evil and harm; from sin; from the wiles and assaults of the devil; from your wrath, and from eternal damnation,
Good Lord, deliver us.

From all spiritual blindness; from pride, boasting, and hypocrisy; from envy, hatred, and malice, and all failure to love others,
Good Lord, deliver us.

From all disordered and sinful feelings; and from all the deceits of the world, the flesh and the devil,
Good Lord, deliver us.

The Litany

From lightning and storm; from earthquake, fire and flood; from plague, disease and famine; from war and murder, and from dying unprepared,
Good Lord, deliver us.

From all treason, sedition, secret conspiracy, and rebellion; from all false doctrine, heresy and schism; from hardness of heart and contempt for your word and commandments,
Good Lord, deliver us.

By the mystery of your holy Incarnation, by your holy birth and circumcision; by your baptism, fasting and temptation,
Good Lord, deliver us.

By your agony and bloody sweat, by your cross and passion; by your precious death and burial; by your glorious resurrection and ascension; and by the coming of the Holy Spirit,
Good Lord, deliver us.

In times of trouble and in times of prosperity; in the hour of death and on the day of judgment,
Good Lord, deliver us.

We, who are sinners, pray that you hear us, Lord God. May it please you to govern and guide your holy, catholic Church in the way of righteousness;
Hear us, good Lord.

The Litany

May it please you to bless and keep in safety all Christian rulers and judges, giving them grace to administer justice and to maintain truth;
Hear us, good Lord.

May it please you to enlighten the minds of all Bishops, Priests, and Deacons, with true knowledge and understanding of your holy Word, so that in their preaching and living they may declare it and show its truth;
Hear us, good Lord.

May it please you to send laborers into your harvest;
Hear us, good Lord.

May it please you to bless and keep all your people;
Hear us, good Lord.

May it please you to give to all nations unity, peace and concord;
Hear us, good Lord.

May it please you to give us hearts to love and worship you, and diligently to keep your commandments;
Hear us, good Lord.

May it please you to give to all your people an increase of grace to listen meekly to your Word, to receive it with pure intention, and to bring forth the fruit of the Spirit in their lives;
Hear us, good Lord.

The Litany

May it please you to bring back into the way of truth all who have erred and are deceived;
Hear us, good Lord.

May it please you to strengthen such as are standing firm in the faith, to comfort and encourage the fainthearted, to raise up those who fall; and finally to beat down Satan under our feet;
Hear us, good Lord.

May it please you to sustain, help and comfort, all who are in danger, need and trouble;
Hear us, good Lord.

May it please you to protect all who travel by land, water, or air, all women in labor, all sick persons and young children; and to show your pity upon all prisoners and captives;
Hear us, good Lord.

May it please you to protect and provide for orphans, widows and all who are desolate and oppressed;
Hear us, good Lord.

May it please you to have mercy upon all people everywhere;
Hear us, good Lord.

May it please you to forgive our enemies, persecutors and slanderers, and to turn their hearts;
Hear us, good Lord.

The Litany

May it please you to give and preserve for our use the fruits of the earth in season, so that in due time we may enjoy them;
Hear us, good Lord.

May it please you to give us true repentance; to forgive our sin, negligence and ignorance; to endue us with the grace of your Holy Spirit and to conform our lives according to your holy Word;
Hear us, good Lord.

Son of God, we pray you to hear us
Son of God, we pray you to hear us.

Lamb of God, you who take away the sin of the world;
Have mercy on us.

Lamb of God, you who take away the sin of the world;
Grant us your peace.

Christ, hear us.
Christ, hear us.

Lord, have mercy.
Christ, have mercy upon us.

Lord, have mercy.

When The Order for Holy Communion is to follow immediately, then all that here follows may be omitted. At other times the Minister, together with the People, say the Lord's Prayer in either the traditional or contemporary form.

The Litany

Traditional

OUR Father who art in heaven, Hallowed be thy Name, Thy kingdom come, Thy will be done, on earth as it is in heaven. Give us this day our daily bread; And forgive us our trespasses, as we forgive them that trespass against us; And lead us not into temptation, but deliver us from evil. For thine is the kingdom, the power and the glory, forever and ever. Amen.

Contemporary

OUR Father in heaven, hallowed be your name. Your kingdom come, your will be done, on earth as in heaven. Give us today our daily bread. Forgive us our sins as we forgive those who sin against us. Lead us not into temptation but deliver us from evil. For yours is the kingdom, and the power, and the glory, forever and ever. Amen.

The Minister may, at his discretion, omit all that follows, to the Prayer, **Gracious Father in your mercy**, etc.

Minister: O Lord, do not deal with us according to our sins.
People: Neither reward us according to our iniquities.
Minister: Let us pray.

O GOD, our merciful Father, you who do not despise the sighing of a contrite heart nor the desires of those who are sorrowful: In your mercy teach and help us to pray to you whenever we are oppressed by adversity or trouble; and graciously hear us so that by your providence the evils brought against us by the cunning

The Litany

and the mischief of the devil or of human beings, may come to nothing; and grant that we, your servants, being harmed by no persecutions, may give thanks and praise to you in your holy Church; through Jesus Christ our Lord. *Amen.*

Minister and People: O Lord, arise, help, and deliver us for your Name's sake.

Minister: Lord God, we have heard with our ears, and our forebears have told us, the wonderful works you did in their day and in the days before them.

Minister and People: O Lord, arise, help, and deliver us for the sake of your honor.

Minister: Glory be to the Father, and to the Son, and to the Holy Spirit;

People: As it was in the beginning, is now, and shall be forever; world without end. Amen.

Minister: From our enemies defend us, O Christ.

People: Graciously look upon us in our afflictions.

Minister: Regard with pity the sorrow of our hearts.

People: Mercifully forgive the sins of your people.

Minister: Favorably with mercy hear our prayers.

People: Son of David, have mercy upon us.

Minister: Both now and always be ready to hear us, Lord Christ.

People: Graciously hear us, O Lord Christ.

Minister: O Lord, let your mercy descend upon us,

People: As we put our trust in you.

The Litany

GRACIOUS Father, in your mercy, look upon us in our weakness; and, for the glory of your name, turn away from us all those evils which we have deserved: Grant that in all our troubles our whole trust and confidence may be in you; and that we may always seek to serve you in holiness and purity of life, to your honor and glory; through our only Mediator and Advocate, Jesus Christ our Lord. *Amen.*

A Prayer of St. Chrysostom

ALMIGHTY God, you who have given us grace at this time to bring before you in one mind our common supplications, and have promised that when two or three are gathered together in your Name you will grant their requests: Fulfill now, O Lord, the desires and petitions of your servants in ways that are best for them, granting us in this world knowledge of your truth, and in the world to come life everlasting. *Amen.*

The Grace, 2 Corinthians 13:14

THE grace of our Lord Jesus Christ, and the love of God, and the fellowship of the Holy Spirit, be with us all evermore. *Amen.*

The Athanasian Creed or Quicunque Vult

Introduction

This Creed or Statement of Faith has been widely used in the West since the early Middle Ages, and is an indispensable statement of the basic dogma of the Holy Trinity and of the Person of Jesus Christ, Incarnate Son of the Father. It is omitted from the American BCP of 1928, but is in the English of 1662 and the Canadian of 1962. It is presented here in full with the warnings against damnation with which it originally began and ended.

WHOEVER desires to be saved must above all things hold the Catholic Faith. Unless a person keeps it in its entirety inviolate, he or she will certainly perish eternally.

Now this is the Catholic Faith that we worship one God in Trinity and Trinity in Unity, without either confusing the Persons or dividing the Substance. For there is one Person of the Father, another of the Son and another of the Holy Spirit, but the Godhead of the Father, the Son and the Holy Spirit is one, their glory is equal and their majesty co-eternal.

Such as the Father is, such is the Son, such also the Holy Spirit. The Father is increate, the Son increate, and the Holy Spirit increate. The Father is infinite, the Son infinite, and the Holy Spirit infinite. The Father is eternal, the Son eternal, and the Holy Spirit eternal. Yet there are not three eternals but one Eternal, just as there are not three increates or three infinites, but one

The Athanasian Creed

Increate and one Infinite. In the same way the Father is almighty, the Son almighty, and the Holy Spirit almighty; yet there are not three almighties, but one Almighty.

Thus the Father is God, the Son is God, and the Holy Spirit is God; and yet there are not three Gods but one God. Thus the Father is Lord, the Son is Lord, and the Holy Spirit is Lord; and yet there are not three Lords but one Lord. Because even as we are obliged by Christian truth to acknowledge each Person separately both God and Lord, so we are forbidden by the Catholic religion to say that there are three Gods and three Lords.

The Father is from none, not made, nor created nor begotten. The Son is from the Father alone, not made, nor created, but begotten. The Holy Spirit is from the Father and the Son, not made nor created but proceeding. So there is one Father, not three Fathers; one Son, not three Sons; one Holy Spirit, not three Holy Spirits. And in this Trinity there is nothing before or after, nothing greater or less, but all three Persons are coeternal with each other and coequal. So that in all things, as has already been stated, both Trinity in Unity and Unity in Trinity must be worshipped. Anyone who desires to be saved should think thus of the Holy Trinity.

Further, it is necessary in order to receive everlasting salvation faithfully to believe in the Incarnation of our Lord Jesus Christ. Now the right faith is that we should believe and confess that our Lord Jesus Christ, the Son of God, is equally both God and man.

The Athanasian Creed

He is God from the Father's Being, begotten before time; and he is man from his mother's being, born in time. Perfect God, perfect man composed of a rational soul and human flesh, equal to the Father in respect of his divinity, less than the Father in respect of his humanity.

Who, although he is God and man, is nevertheless not two, but one Christ. He is one, however, not by the transformation of his divinity into flesh, but by the taking up of his humanity into God; one certainly not by confusion of substance, but by oneness of Person. For just as the rational soul and flesh are a single man, so God and man are a single Christ.

Who suffered for our salvation, descended into hell, rose from the dead, ascended to heaven, sat down at the right hand of the Father, from where he will come to judge the living and the dead; at whose coming all persons will rise again with their bodies, and will render an account of their deeds; and those who have done good will go into everlasting life, and those who have done evil into everlasting fire.

This is the Catholic Faith. Unless a person believes it faithfully and steadfastly he or she will not be able to be saved.

An Order for Compline

The Minister, ordained or lay, begins,

THE Lord Almighty grant us a quiet night and a perfect end. Amen.

Minister: O God, make speed to save us;

Answer: O Lord, make haste to help us.

Minister: Glory be to the Father, and to the Son, and to the Holy Spirit;

Answer: As it was in the beginning, is now, and shall be forever; world without end. Amen.

Minister: Let us praise the Lord;

Answer: The Lord's Name be praised.

Here is said or sung one or more of the following Psalms: 4, 31:1–6; 91, 134 or any other suitable Psalm.

Then is read one of the following Lessons or another suitable portion of Scripture: Jeremiah 14:9 & 22; Matthew 11: 28–30; Hebrews 13:20–21; 1 Peter 3:8–9a

After the reading all say:

Thanks be to God.

Then may be said the following:

Minister: Into your hands, O Lord, I commend my spirit;

Answer: Into your hands, O Lord, I commend my spirit.

Minister: For you have redeemed me, O Lord God of truth;

Answer: I commend my spirit.

Compline

Minister: Glory be to the Father, and to the Son, and to the Holy Spirit.

Answer: Into your hands, O Lord, I commend my spirit.

Here may follow this traditional Hymn.

Te lucis ante terminum

To you before the end of day,
Creator of the world, we pray:
In love unfailing hear our prayer,
Enfold us in your watchful care.

Keep all disturbing dreams away,
And hold the evil foe at bay.
Repose untroubled let us find
For soul and body, heart and mind.

Almighty Father, this accord
Through Jesus Christ, your Son, our Lord:
Who reigns with you eternally
In your blest Spirit's unity. Amen.

Minister: Guard us as the pupil in your eye;
Answer: Hide us in the shadow of your wings.
Antiphon: Preserve us, Lord, awaking, and guard us sleeping, that awake we may watch with Christ, and sleeping we may rest in peace

In the Easter season add: **Alleluia, Alleluia, Alleluia.**

Compline

Lord, now you are letting your servant depart in peace, according to your word;

For my eyes have seen your salvation, that you have prepared in the sight of all peoples;

A light for revelation to the Gentiles, and for glory to your people Israel.

Glory be to the Father, and to the Son, and to the Holy Spirit:

As it was in the beginning, is now, and shall be forever; world without end. Amen.

Antiphon: Preserve us, O Lord, awaking, and guard us sleeping, that awake we may watch with Christ, and sleeping we may rest in peace

Then the Apostles' Creed is said by the Minister and the People, standing.

I believe in God the Father Almighty, creator of heaven and earth. And I believe in Jesus Christ, his only Son, our Lord. He was conceived by the Holy Spirit and born of the Virgin Mary. He suffered under Pontius Pilate, was crucified, died and was buried. He descended to the dead. On the third day he rose again. He ascended into heaven and sits at the right hand of God the Father Almighty. From there he shall come to judge the living and the dead. I believe in the Holy Spirit, the holy Catholic Church, the communion of saints, the forgiveness of sins, the resurrection of the body and the life everlasting. Amen.

Compline

Minister: Let us pray.
Lord, have mercy upon us.
Christ, *have mercy upon us.*
Lord have mercy upon us.

Traditional

Our Father who art in heaven, Hallowed be thy Name, Thy kingdom come, Thy will be done, on earth as it is in heaven. Give us this day our daily bread; And forgive us our trespasses, as we forgive them that trespass against us; And lead us not into temptation, but deliver us from evil. For thine is the kingdom, the power and the glory, forever and ever. Amen.

Contemporary

Our Father in heaven, hallowed be your name. Your kingdom come, your will be done, on earth as in heaven. Give us today our daily bread. Forgive us our sins as we forgive those who sin against us. Lead us not into temptation but deliver us from evil. For yours is the kingdom, and the power, and the glory, forever and ever. Amen.

Minister: Blessed are you, Lord God of our fathers;
Answer: To be praised and glorified above all forever.
Minister: Let us bless the Father, the Son, and the Holy Spirit.
Answer: Let us praise him and proclaim his greatness forever.
Minister: Blessed are you, O Lord, in the heavens above;
Answer: To be praised and glorified above all forever.

Compline

Minister: The Almighty and most merciful Lord guard us and give us his blessing.

Answer: Amen.

Then the Minister and people say together both the Confession and Prayer for Forgiveness.

WE confess to God Almighty, the Father, the Son and the Holy Spirit, that we have sinned in thought, word and deed, through our own grievous fault. Almighty God, have mercy upon us, forgive us all our sins and deliver us from all evil, confirm and strengthen us in all goodness, and bring us to everlasting life; through Jesus Christ our Lord. Amen.

When a Priest is present he says,

MAY the Almighty and merciful Lord grant to you pardon and remission of all your sins, time for amendment of life, and the grace and comfort of the Holy Spirit. *Amen.*

Then the following is said:

Minister: Will you not turn again and revive us?
Answer: That your people may rejoice in you?
Minister: O Lord, show your mercy upon us;
Answer: And grant us your salvation.
Minister: Be pleased, O Lord, to keep us this night without sin.
Answer: O Lord, have mercy upon us, have mercy upon us.
Minister: O Lord, hear our prayer;
Answer: And let our cry come unto you.

Compline

One or both of the following two Collects is said; and the Collect of the Day may also be used.

Lighten our darkness, Lord, we pray, and by your great mercy defend us from all perils and dangers of this night, for the love of your only Son, our Savior Jesus Christ. *Amen.*

Visit, O Lord, this place and drive from it all the snares of the enemy; let your holy angels dwell here to preserve us in peace; and may your blessing be upon us always; through Jesus Christ our Lord. *Amen.*

Minister: We will lie down in peace and take our rest;
Answer: For it is you alone, Lord, who make us dwell in safety.
Minister: The Lord be with you.
Answer: And with your spirit.
Minister: Let us bless the Lord.
Answer: Thanks be to God.

The Almighty and merciful Lord, the Father, the Son and the Holy Spirit, bless and preserve us. *Amen.*

The Order for the Holy Communion

Introduction

In order profitably to enter into the fullness of the doctrine and style of this biblically-based liturgy, one needs to use it in full—that is, with its own Collects and Eucharistic Lectionary. In The Book of Common Prayer (editions of 1662; 1928; 1962) the printing of the Collect, Epistle and Gospel for each Sunday and holy Day takes up many pages, and they are a crucial part of the BCP. They link the BCP with the medieval Latin use and via this with late Patristic use, and so there is continuity in use of Scripture in the Eucharist and the doctrine conveyed by this ordered reading of Holy Scripture. The Eucharistic Lectionary has fifth century origins and reaches its mid-point with Trinity Sunday, the celebration of The Triune God.

While this Service is open to all, only those who are baptized in the name of the Father, the Son and the Holy Spirit, and are duly prepared in mind and heart, should receive Holy Communion. Any person who has doubts about worthiness to communicate is urged to seek godly advice and direction as soon as possible.

The Celebrant is the Bishop or the Priest, assisted where appropriate by a Deacon and licensed laity. They wear only such vestments as are allowed by canon law.

The Holy Table is covered by a white linen cloth.

This Service may be preceded by either Morning or Evening Prayer and also by the Litany.

The version of the Bible recommended for use is the English Standard Version or the Revised Standard Version.

If the Service is not preceded by Morning or Evening Prayer, then it is recommended that a reading from the Old Testament and the praying of a Psalm be inserted after the Collect and before the appointed Epistle and Gospel. The provision of Collect,

Holy Communion

Epistle and Gospel, with an Old Testament Lesson and Psalm for each Sunday, Festival and Holy Day is found below, after the text of the Service.

There is no provision in the English BCP 1662, or its edited forms as USA 1928 or Canada 1962, for a public, expressive form of "passing of the peace." The "Peace of God" itself is communicated by receiving the Sacrament and by the first part of the Blessing at the end of the Service, which begins, "The Peace of God which passes all understanding…" However, Canada 1962 actually has the "Peace" in a traditional, medieval, Western form, as a verbal exchange between the Celebrant and the congregation while the people kneel, as in the old Roman Rite. If the people are used to a modern, expressive form of "passing of the peace," and desire it, then the Minister may at his discretion add this to begin the Service or at the notices.

It is important to note that the words – "The Lord be with you" "And with your spirit" – are not a modern type of expressive greeting as such. They are more like a prayer, where the presence of the Lord with his people is being affirmed by the Minister, and, in turn, the people pray that the spiritual gift given to him in ordination will be aroused, so that the Celebration will be in spirit and in truth, and thus acceptable to the Lord.

Many of the original rubrics have been left out of this Service. This means that there is greater local freedom for use of licensed laity, congregational participation, and singing of psalms, hymns and spiritual songs.

For the second half of the Service, the Ministry of the Sacrament, there is a choice from three Orders, the English, the American, and the Canadian. These have the same textual material but use it in different ways, and, thereby, illustrate the major ways that the text of the Eucharist has been organized and celebrated in the classic tradition of Common Prayer in the Anglican Way from 1662 to the present.

Holy Communion

Holy Communion

The Minister may welcome the people and a hymn may be sung.

The Lord's Prayer may be said by the Minister alone, who then proceeds by saying,

The Lord be with you
People: And with your spirit.

ALMIGHTY God, unto whom all hearts are open, all desires known, and from whom no secrets are hidden, cleanse the thoughts of our hearts by the inspiration of your Holy Spirit, that we may perfectly love you, and worthily magnify your holy name, through Christ our Lord. *Amen.*

At least once a month, the Minister reads aloud the Ten Commandments and the congregation asks God's forgiveness for their transgressions and grace to obey God's laws in the future. The words in brackets may be omitted. On other occasions, he uses the summary of the Law as given by the Lord Jesus Christ.

GOD spoke these words and said: I am the Lord your God [who brought you out of the land of Egypt, out of the house of slavery]; you shall have no other gods before me.

You shall not make for yourself a carved image, or any likeness of anything that is in heaven above, or that is in the earth below, or that is in the water under the earth.

You shall not bow down to them or serve them, [for I the LORD your God am a jealous God, visiting the

Holy Communion

iniquity of the fathers on the children to the third and fourth generation of those who hate me, but showing steadfast love to thousands of those who love me and keep my commandments].

You shall not take the name of the Lord your God in vain, [for the Lord will not hold him guiltless who takes his name in vain].

Remember the Sabbath day, to keep it holy. [Six days you shall labor and do all your work, but the seventh day is a Sabbath to the Lord your God. On it you shall not do any work, you, or your son, or your daughter, your male servant, or your female servant, or your livestock, or the sojourner who is within your gates. For in six days the Lord made heaven and earth, the sea, and all that is in them, and rested the seventh day. Therefore the Lord blessed the Sabbath day and made it holy.]

People: Lord, have mercy on us, and write these laws in our hearts.

Honor your father and your mother, [that your days may be long in the land that the Lord your God is giving you].

You shall not murder.

You shall not commit adultery.

You shall not steal.

You shall not bear false witness against your neighbor.

You shall not covet [your neighbor's house, you shall not covet your neighbor's wife, or his male servant, or

Holy Communion

his female servant, or his ox, or his donkey, or anything that is your neighbor's].

People: Lord, have mercy on us, and write these laws in our hearts.

Or the Summary of the Law.

Our Lord Jesus Christ said:

"Hear O Israel, the Lord our God is one. And you shall love the Lord your God with all your heart and with all your soul and with all your mind and with all your strength. The second is this: You shall love your neighbor as yourself. There is no other commandment greater than these."

Here may follow either this, or the response following:

Lord, have mercy upon us.
Christ, have mercy upon us.
Lord, have mercy upon us.

People: Lord, have mercy upon us, and write these laws in our hearts.

The Minister says the Collect of the day.

A lesson from the Old Testament may be read. After it the reader says, **This is the word of the Lord**, and the congregation responds with, **Thanks be to God.**

A psalm, hymn, canticle, or anthem may be said or sung following each or any of the readings.

The appointed Epistle is introduced as follows: **The Epistle is written in the _ chapter of _ beginning at verse _ .** It is

Holy Communion

concluded with the same words as the reading from the Old Testament, **Thanks be to God.**

The congregation stands for the Gospel which is introduced as follows:

The holy Gospel of our Lord Jesus Christ is written in the _ chapter of the Gospel according to Saint _ , beginning at verse _ .

The people respond: **Glory to you, Lord Christ.**

At the end of the Gospel, the reader says: **This is the Gospel of the Lord.**

The people respond: **Praise to you, Lord Christ.**

The Sermon may be preached here or after the Creed.

The Congregation stands for the Creed.

I BELIEVE in one God, the Father Almighty, maker of heaven and earth, and of all things visible and invisible.

I believe in one Lord Jesus Christ, the only Son of God, begotten of the Father before all ages, God from God, Light from Light, true God from true God, begotten, not made, of one Being with the Father; through him all things were made. For us and for our salvation he came down from heaven, and was incarnate from the Holy Spirit and the Virgin Mary, and was made man. For our sake he was crucified under Pontius Pilate; he suffered death and was buried. On the third day he rose again in accordance with the Scriptures; he ascended into heaven and is seated at the right hand of the Father.

Holy Communion

He shall come again in glory to judge the living and the dead, and his kingdom will have no end.

I believe in the Holy Spirit, the Lord, the giver of life, who proceeds from the Father and the Son, who with the Father and the Son is worshipped and glorified, who has spoken through the prophets. I believe in one, holy, catholic, and apostolic Church. I acknowledge one baptism for the forgiveness of sins. I look for the resurrection of the dead, and the life of the world to come. Amen.

> The Sermon is preached here if not already preached immediately after the Gospel.
>
> The Notices are given and forthcoming holy days and fast days are announced.
>
> Sentences from Scripture concerning the joy and duty of giving unto the Lord are read before the Offering is taken up and received.
>
> The holy Table is prepared for Communion and an anthem, spiritual songs or hymns may be sung.
>
> Then follows the Prayer of Intercession.

ALMIGHTY and ever-living God, you who by your holy Apostle Paul have taught us by your holy Word to offer prayers and petitions, and to give thanks, for all people: We humbly ask you most mercifully to receive our prayers which we offer to your divine Majesty, asking you to inspire continually the universal Church with the spirit of truth, unity and harmony, and

Holy Communion

to grant that all who confess your holy Name may agree in the truth of your holy Word, and live in unity and godly love.

We pray that you will lead the nations of the world into the ways of righteousness and peace, and guide their leaders in wisdom and justice to act for the good of all people. Bless, especially, we ask, [*here both the leaders of the nation and locality are named*]. Grant that they may impartially administer justice, restrain wickedness and vice, maintain true religion, and uphold integrity and truth.

And we ask you in your goodness, Lord, to comfort and sustain all who in this short life on earth are in trouble, sorrow, need, sickness, or any other adversity.

Give grace, heavenly Father, to all bishops and other ministers [especially *N.* our bishop and *N.* our clergy], that, by their life and teaching, they may set forth your true, life-giving Word, and rightly and duly administer your holy Sacraments. And to all your people, give your heavenly grace, and especially to this congregation, that they may receive your word with reverent and obedient hearts, and also serve you in holiness and righteousness all the days of their life.

We also bless your holy name for all your servants who have died in the faith of Christ. Give us grace to follow their good examples, that with them we may be partakers of your heavenly kingdom.

Grant all this, Father, for Jesus Christ's sake, our only

Holy Communion

Mediator and Advocate, who lives and reigns with you in the unity of the Holy Spirit, now and forever. Amen.

> As an alternative to this Prayer, a series of biddings, led by the Minister or a lay person, may be used. After each bidding the leader says: **Lord in your mercy,** and the congregation responds, **Hear our prayer.** At the end, the Minister says, **Merciful Father**, and the congregation responds, **Accept our prayers for the sake of your Son, our Savior Jesus Christ. Amen.**

> The Prayer being ended, the Minister reads the following Exhortation, at least once a month.

Fellow baptized Christians, it is appropriate that we recall how St Paul, in writing to the church in Corinth, urged Christians to examine themselves before presuming to eat the holy Bread and drink from the holy Cup of the Lord's Supper. If we receive the holy Sacrament with truly penitent and believing hearts, then we spiritually eat the body of Christ and drink his blood; then also we dwell in Christ and Christ in us, for we are one with Christ and he with us. However, if we receive the Sacrament unworthily, then we will be guilty of profaning the body and blood of the Lord.

Therefore, brothers and sisters, examine yourselves, and repent of your past sins; have a lively and steadfast faith in Christ our Savior; amend your lives, and be in perfect love with all people; then you will be worthy partakers of this holy Sacrament. And, above all things, give humble and hearty thanks to God the Father, the Son, and the Holy Spirit, for the redemption of the

Holy Communion

world by the death of our Savior Christ, who is both God and man.

He humbled himself, even to the death on the Cross, for us unworthy sinners, who were in darkness and under the shadow of death; that he might make us the children of God and exalt us to everlasting life. And so that we should always remember both the exceeding great love of our Master and only Savior Jesus Christ, who died for us, and also the benefits, too many to be numbered, which he obtained for us by the shedding of his blood, he has instituted and ordained holy mysteries, as pledges of his love and for a continual remembrance of his death, to our great and endless support and comfort. To him, therefore, with the Father and the Holy Spirit, let us give, as we are required, continual thanks; let us submit ourselves wholly to his holy will and good pleasure, and seek to serve him in true holiness and righteousness all the days of our life. *Amen*.

Then the Minister says to all who intend to receive the Holy Communion:

IF you truly and sincerely repent of your sins, are reconciled and at peace with your neighbors, and intend to lead a new life, following the commandments of God and walking from this day forward in his holy ways; draw near with faith, take this holy Sacrament to strengthen and comfort you, and make your humble confession to Almighty God.

Holy Communion

A pause for self-examination may be observed. All then say this General Confession, kneeling.

ALMIGHTY God, Father of our Lord Jesus Christ, maker of all things, judge of all people, we acknowledge and confess our many sins, which we have committed from time to time by thought, word and deed against your divine Majesty, provoking most justly your righteous anger against us. We earnestly repent, and are deeply sorry for all our wrongdoings. The memory of them grieves us and the burden of them is too great for us to bear. Have mercy upon us, most merciful Father.

For your Son our Lord Jesus Christ's sake, forgive us all that is past and grant from this time forward we may serve and please you in newness of life, to the honor and glory of your name; through Jesus Christ our Lord. *Amen.*

The Minister declares God's forgiveness.

ALMIGHTY God, our heavenly Father, who in his great mercy has promised forgiveness of sins to all those who with sincere repentance and true faith turn to him: Have mercy on you, pardon and deliver you from all your sins, confirm and strengthen you in all goodness, and bring you to everlasting life, through Jesus Christ our Lord. *Amen.*

Hear the words of assurance addressed by our Lord Jesus Christ to those who truly turn to him:

Holy Communion

Come to me, all who labor and are heavy laden, and I will give you rest. *Matthew 11:28*

God so loved the world that he gave his only Son, that whoever believes in him should not perish but have eternal life. *John 3:16*

Hear also what St Paul said:

The saying is trustworthy and deserving of full acceptance, that Christ Jesus came into the world to save sinners. *1 Timothy 1:15*

And hear what St John said:

If anyone does sin, we have an advocate with the Father, Jesus Christ the righteous. He is the propitiation for our sins, and not for ours only but also for the sins of the whole world. *1 John 2:1*

After a brief moment for reflection, the Priest begins the Preface of the Prayer of Consecration.

Priest: The Lord be with you
People. And with your spirit.
Priest. Lift up your hearts.
People: We lift them to the Lord.
Priest: Let us give thanks to the Lord our God.
People: It is right to give him thanks and praise.

Priest.

Holy Father, almighty and everlasting God, Creator and Preserver of all things, it is good and right at all times, and in all places, to give you thanks and praise:

Holy Communion

A Proper Preface normally follows here if one is appointed. Otherwise the Priest continues,

THEREFORE with angels and archangels, and with all the company of heaven, we proclaim and magnify your glorious Name, forever praising you, and saying:

Priest and people together.

HOLY, HOLY, HOLY, Lord God of hosts, heaven and earth are full of your glory. Glory be to you, O Lord most high. *Amen.*

Proper Prefaces

On Christmas Day, and during the Octave thereof, and on the Feast of the Annunciation.

BECAUSE you gave your only Son Jesus Christ to be born for us. By the presence and work of the Holy Spirit, he was made man, born of the Virgin Mary, his mother, but without sin, in order to make us clean from all sin. Therefore…

After the Octave of Christmas to the Eve of the Epiphany, and on the Feasts of the Purification and Transfiguration.

BECAUSE in the mystery of the Word made flesh, you have caused a new light to shine in our hearts, to give the knowledge of your glory in the face of your Son, Jesus Christ our Lord. Therefore…

On the Epiphany, and seven days after.

THROUGH Jesus Christ our Lord, who in our mortal flesh, revealed his glory, that he might bring us out of darkness into his own marvelous light. Therefore…

Holy Communion

On Passion Sunday, and until Maundy Thursday inclusive.

For the redemption of the world by the death and passion of our Savior Christ, God and Man; who humbled himself, even to death upon the Cross for us sinners, and who lay in darkness and the shadow of death; that he might make us children of God and exalt us to everlasting life. Therefore...

On Easter Day, and until the Eve of Ascension Day.

But above all we must praise you for the glorious resurrection of your Son Jesus Christ our Lord: for he is the Passover Lamb, who was offered for us and has taken away the sin of the world; who by his death has destroyed death; and by his rising to life again has restored everlasting life to us. Therefore...

On Ascension Day, and until the Eve of Whitsunday (Pentecost) inclusive.

Through your most dearly loved Son Jesus Christ our Lord, who after his glorious resurrection appeared to the apostles, and in their sight ascended into heaven to prepare a place for us, so that where he is, there we might also ascend and reign with him in glory. Therefore...

On Whitsunday (Pentecost), and six days after.

Through Jesus Christ our Lord, according to whose sure promise the Holy Spirit came down from heaven upon the disciples and apostles, to teach them

Holy Communion

and to lead them into all truth; giving them both the gift of tongues, and also boldness with fervent zeal to preach the Gospel to all nations, by which we have been brought out of darkness and error into the clear light and true knowledge of you and of your Son Jesus Christ. Therefore…

On Trinity Sunday and at any time during the Trinity season.

WHOM with your co-eternal Son and Holy Spirit, we confess to be one God, one Lord, in Trinity of Persons and in Unity of Substance. For what we believe of your glory, O Father, we also believe of the Son and of the Holy Spirit, without any difference or inequality. Therefore…

On All Saints' Day, and other Festivals of Saints.

WHO, in the multitude of your saints, have surrounded us with so great a cloud of witnesses, that rejoicing in their fellowship we may run patiently the race that is set before us, and, together with them, may receive the crown of glory that does not fade away. Therefore…

On any Sunday for which no other Proper Preface is appointed.

THROUGH Jesus Christ our Lord; for he is the true High Priest, who has washed us from our sins, and has made us to be a kingdom of priests unto you, our God and Father. Therefore…

Holy Communion

After each of these Prefaces the following shall be said:

Therefore with angels and archangels, and with all the company of heaven, we proclaim and magnify your glorious name, forever praising you, and saying:

Priest and people together

Holy, Holy, Holy, Lord God of hosts, heaven and earth are full of your glory. Glory be to you, O Lord most high. Amen.

[Either here or immediately before the Communion may be said or sung: **Blessed is he who comes in the name of the Lord. Hosannah in the highest.**]

From here to the end of the Service there are three options: (a) The English Order of 1662, and (b) The American Order of 1928, and (c) The Canadian Order of 1962.

The English Order, 1662

The Minister, kneeling down at the Lord's Table, says with all who intend to receive the Holy Communion, this Prayer.

We do not presume to come to this your table, merciful Lord, trusting in our own righteousness, but in your abundant and great mercies. We are not worthy so much as to gather up the crumbs under your table. But you are the same Lord, who always delights in showing mercy. Grant us, therefore, gracious Lord, so to eat the flesh of your dear Son Jesus Christ and to drink his blood, that our sinful bodies may be made clean by his body, and our souls washed through his most precious blood, and that we may evermore dwell in him, and he in us. Amen.

Holy Communion

The Minister standing at the holy Table says the Prayer of Consecration.

Almighty God, our heavenly Father, who, in your tender mercy, gave your only Son our Savior Jesus Christ to suffer death upon the Cross for our redemption: who made there (by his one oblation of himself once offered) a full satisfaction, perfect self-offering and sufficient sacrifice, for the sins of the whole world; and instituted, and in his holy gospel commanded us to continue, a perpetual memory of his precious death, until he comes again.

Hear us, merciful Father, we humbly pray, and grant that we receiving these gifts of your creation, this bread and this wine, according to your Son our Savior Jesus Christ's holy institution, in remembrance of his death and passion, may be partakers of his most blessed Body and Blood: who, in the same night that he was betrayed, [*here the Minister takes the paten into his hands*] took Bread; and, when he had given you thanks, [*here he breaks the bread*] he broke it and gave it to his disciples, saying: Take, eat; [*here he lays his hand over all the bread*]: this is my Body which is given for you: do this in remembrance of me.

In the same way, after supper, [*here he takes the chalice*] he took the Cup; and, when he had given thanks, he gave it to them, saying: Drink this, all of you, for [*here he lays his hand on every vessel in which there is wine to be consecrated*] this is my Blood of the new covenant, which is shed for you and for many for the

Holy Communion

forgiveness of sins. Do this, as often as you drink it, in remembrance of me.

People. Amen.

> The Minister receives Communion and then delivers the same to the clergy and lay assistants. This done, the congregation comes forward in an orderly manner to receive Holy Communion as they kneel. The following words of administration are used.

THE body of our Lord Jesus Christ which was given for you, preserve your body and soul to everlasting life. Take and eat this in remembrance that Christ died for you and feed on him in your heart by faith with thanksgiving.

THE blood of our Lord Jesus Christ, which was shed for you, preserve your body and soul to everlasting life. Drink this in remembrance that Christ's blood was shed for you and be thankful.

> What remains of the consecrated bread and wine, and which is not required for the communion of the sick after the Service, may be consumed reverently now or at the end of the service.

> In the time for receiving, Communion hymns, spiritual songs or anthems may be used, such as **Agnus Dei.**

> The Minister calls the congregation to join in the Lord's Prayer.

Holy Communion

Traditional

Our Father who art in heaven, Hallowed be thy Name, Thy kingdom come, Thy will be done, on earth as it is in heaven. Give us this day our daily bread; And forgive us our trespasses, as we forgive them that trespass against us; And lead us not into temptation, but deliver us from evil. For thine is the kingdom, the power and the glory, forever and ever. Amen.

Contemporary

Our Father in heaven, hallowed be your name. Your kingdom come, your will be done, on earth as in heaven. Give us today our daily bread. Forgive us our sins as we forgive those who sin against us. Lead us not into temptation but deliver us from evil. For yours is the kingdom, and the power, and the glory, forever and ever. Amen.

The Minister alone or with the people says one or both of the following two prayers.

Gracious Lord and heavenly Father, we your servants wholly desire that in your fatherly goodness you will mercifully accept this sacrifice of praise and thanksgiving. Grant that, by the merits and death of your Son Jesus Christ, and through faith in his blood, with your whole Church we may receive forgiveness of our sins and all other benefits of his passion. Here we offer and present to you, ourselves, our souls and bodies, to be a reasonable, holy, and living sacrifice. Fill us all, who share in this Holy Communion, with your grace and heavenly benediction. And although we

Holy Communion

are unworthy, through our many sins, to offer to you any sacrifice, yet we pray that you will accept this, the duty and service we owe. Do not weigh our merits but pardon our offenses, through Jesus Christ our Lord; by whom and with whom, in the unity of the Holy Spirit, all honor and glory are yours, Father Almighty, forever and ever. Amen.

Almighty and ever-living God, we most sincerely thank you that you graciously feed us, who have duly received these holy mysteries, with the spiritual food of the most precious Body and Blood of your Son, our Savior Jesus Christ. We also thank you that you have assured us in this Sacrament of your favor and goodness towards us, and that we are true members of the mystical body of your Son, the blessed company of all faithful people, and are also heirs, through hope, of your eternal kingdom, by the merits of the most precious death of your dear Son. And we humbly ask you, heavenly Father, so to assist us with your grace, that we may continue in that holy fellowship, and do all such good works as you have prepared for us to walk in; through Jesus Christ our Lord, to whom with you and the Holy Spirit be all honor and glory, forever and ever. Amen.

This hymn of praise or another is now said or sung by all.

Glory be to God on high, and on earth peace, good will towards men. We praise you, we bless you, we worship you, we glorify you, we give thanks to you for

Holy Communion

your great glory, O Lord God, heavenly King, God the Father Almighty.

O Lord, the only-begotten Son, Jesus Christ; O Lord God, Lamb of God, Son of the Father; you who take away the sin of the world, have mercy on us. You who take away the sin of the world, receive our prayer. You who sit at the right hand of God the Father, have mercy on us.

For you only are holy; you only are the Lord; you only, O Christ, with the Holy Spirit, are most high in the glory of God the Father. Amen.

The Minister concludes the service with the Blessing.

THE peace of God, which passes all understanding, keep your hearts and minds in the knowledge and love of God, and of his Son Jesus Christ our Lord: and the blessing of God Almighty, the Father, the Son and the Holy Spirit, be among you, and remain with you always. *Amen.*

The American Order, 1928

ALL glory be to you, Almighty God, our heavenly Father, who, in your tender mercy, gave your only Son Jesus Christ to suffer death upon the Cross for our redemption: who made there (by his one oblation of himself once offered) a full satisfaction, perfect self-offering and sufficient sacrifice, for the sins of the whole world; and instituted, and in his holy gospel commanded us to continue, a perpetual memory of his precious death until he comes again.

Holy Communion

For in the night that he was betrayed [*here the Priest takes the paten into his hands*], he took bread; and when he had given you thanks, [*here he breaks the bread*] he broke it and gave it to his disciples, saying: Take, eat, [*here he lays his hand over all the bread*] this is my Body which is given for you: Do this in remembrance of me. In the same way, after supper, [*here he takes the chalice*] he took the Cup; and when he had given thanks, he gave it to them, saying: Drink this, all of you, for [*here he lays his hand on every vessel in which there is wine to be consecrated*] this is my Blood of the new covenant which is shed for you and for many for the forgiveness of sins; Do this, as often as you drink it, in remembrance of me.

[*The Oblation*] And so, O Lord and heavenly Father, according to the institution of your dearly loved Son, our Savior Jesus Christ, we, your humble servants, do celebrate and make before your Divine Majesty, which we now offer to you, the memorial your Son has commanded us to make; and, as we do so, we remember his blessed passion and precious death, his mighty resurrection and glorious ascension; and we offer to you most sincere thanks for the benefits without number, procured for us by the same.

[*The Invocation*] And we most humbly ask you, merciful Father, to hear us, and of your almighty goodness, graciously to bless and sanctify, with your Word and Holy Spirit, these your gifts from creation of bread and wine; that we, receiving them according to your Son

Holy Communion

our Savior Jesus Christ's holy institution, and remembering his death and passion, may be partakers of his most blessed Body and Blood.

And we sincerely desire that in your fatherly goodness you will mercifully accept this sacrifice of praise and thanksgiving. We humbly ask you to grant that, by the merits and death of your Son Jesus Christ, and through faith in his blood, we and your whole Church may receive forgiveness of our sins and all other benefits of his passion. Here we offer and present to you, Lord, ourselves, our souls and bodies, to be a reasonable, holy, and living sacrifice unto you; and we sincerely ask you to grant that we, and all others who shall be partakers of this Holy Communion, may worthily receive the most precious Body and Blood of your Son Jesus Christ, be filled with your grace and heavenly blessing, and made one body with him, that he may dwell in us and we in him.

And although we are unworthy, through our many sins, to offer to you any sacrifice, yet we humbly ask you to accept this our required duty and service; not weighing our merits but pardoning our offences, through Jesus Christ our Lord; by whom, and with whom, in the unity of the Holy Spirit, all honor and glory be given to you, Father Almighty, forever and ever. *Amen.*

And now, as our Savior Jesus Christ has taught us, so we are bold to say:

Holy Communion

Traditional

OUR Father who art in heaven, Hallowed be thy Name, Thy kingdom come, Thy will be done, on earth as it is in heaven. Give us this day our daily bread; And forgive us our trespasses, as we forgive them that trespass against us; And lead us not into temptation, but deliver us from evil. For thine is the kingdom, the power and the glory, forever and ever. Amen.

Contemporary

OUR Father in heaven, hallowed be your name. Your kingdom come, your will be done, on earth as in heaven. Give us today our daily bread. Forgive us our sins as we forgive those who sin against us. Lead us not into temptation but deliver us from evil. For yours is the kingdom, and the power, and the glory, forever and ever. Amen.

Then the Priest, kneeling down at the Lord's Table, says with all who intend to receive the Holy Communion, this Prayer.

WE do not presume to come to this your table, merciful Lord, trusting in our own righteousness, but in your abundant and great mercies. We are not worthy so much as to gather up the crumbs under your table. But you are the same Lord, who always delights in showing mercy. Grant us, therefore, gracious Lord, so to eat the flesh of your dear Son Jesus Christ and to drink his blood, that our sinful bodies may be made clean by his body, and our souls washed through his most precious blood, and that we may evermore dwell in him, and he in us. Amen.

Holy Communion

The Minister receives Communion and then delivers the same to the clergy and lay assistants. This done, the congregation comes forward in an orderly manner to receive Holy Communion as they kneel. The following words of administration are used.

THE body of our Lord Jesus Christ which was given for you, preserve your body and soul to everlasting life. Take and eat this in remembrance that Christ died for you and feed on him in your heart by faith with thanksgiving.

THE blood of our Lord Jesus Christ, which was shed for you, preserve your body and soul to everlasting life. Drink this in remembrance that Christ's blood was shed for you and be thankful.

What remains of the consecrated bread and wine and which is not required for the communion of the sick after the Service may be consumed reverently now or at the end of the service.

In the time for receiving, Communion hymns, spiritual songs or anthems may be used, such as **Agnus Dei**.

Then is said by the Minister alone or with the people,

ALMIGHTY and ever-living God, we most sincerely thank you that you graciously feed us, who have duly received these holy mysteries, with the spiritual food of the most precious Body and Blood of your Son, our Savior Jesus Christ. We also thank you that you have assured us in this Sacrament of your favor and goodness towards us, and that we are true members of the mystical body of your Son, the blessed company of

Holy Communion

all faithful people, and are also heirs, through hope, of your eternal kingdom, by the merits of the most precious death of your dear Son. And we humbly ask you, heavenly Father, so to assist us with your grace, that we may continue in that holy fellowship, and do all such good works as you have prepared for us to walk in; through Jesus Christ our Lord, to whom with you and the Holy Spirit be given all honor and glory, forever and ever. Amen.

This hymn of praise or another is now said or sung by all.

GLORY be to God on high, and on earth peace, good will towards men. We praise you, we bless you, we worship you, we glorify you, we give thanks to you for your great glory, O Lord God, heavenly King, God the Father Almighty.

O Lord, the only-begotten Son, Jesus Christ; O Lord God, Lamb of God, Son of the Father; you who take away the sin of the world, have mercy on us. You who take away the sin of the world, receive our prayer. You who sit at the right hand of God the Father, have mercy on us.

For you only are holy; you only are the Lord; you only, O Christ, with the Holy Spirit, are most high in the glory of God the Father. Amen.

The Minister concludes the service with the Blessing.

THE peace of God, which passes all understanding, keep your hearts and minds in the knowledge and love of God, and of his Son Jesus Christ our Lord: and

Holy Communion

the blessing of God Almighty, the Father, the Son and the Holy Spirit, be among you, and remain with you always. *Amen.*

The Canadian Order, 1962

BLESSING and glory and thanksgiving be to you, Almighty God, our heavenly Father, who, in your tender mercy, gave your only Son our Savior Jesus Christ to take to himself our human nature, and to suffer death upon the Cross for our redemption: who made there (by his one oblation of himself once offered) a full satisfaction, perfect self-offering and sufficient sacrifice, for the sins of the whole world; and instituted, and in his holy gospel commanded us to continue, a perpetual memorial of his precious death until he comes again.

Hear us, merciful Father, we humbly pray, and grant that we receiving these gifts of your creation, this bread and this wine, according to your Son our Savior Jesus Christ's holy institution, in remembrance of his death and passion, may be partakers of his most blessed Body and Blood: who, in the same night that he was betrayed [*here the Priest takes the paten into his hands*] took bread; and when he had given you thanks, [*here he breaks the bread*] he broke it; and gave it to his disciples, saying: Take, eat, [*here he lays his hand over all the bread*] this is my Body which is given for you: Do this in remembrance of me. In the same way, after supper, [*here he takes the chalice*] he took the Cup; and when he had given thanks, he gave it to them, saying: Drink this, all of you, for [*here he lays his hands on every vessel in*

Holy Communion

which there is wine to be consecrated] this is my Blood of the new Covenant, which is shed for you and for many for the forgiveness of sins: Do this, as often as you drink it, in remembrance of me.

And so, Father, Lord of heaven and earth, we your humble servants, with all your holy Church, remembering the precious death of your beloved Son, his mighty resurrection, his glorious ascension, and looking for his coming again in glory, make before you, in this Sacrament of the holy Bread of eternal life and the Cup of everlasting salvation, the memorial which he has commanded; and we wholly desire your fatherly goodness mercifully to accept this our sacrifice of praise and thanksgiving, as we humbly ask you, by the merits and death of your Son Jesus Christ, and through faith in his Blood, to grant to us and all your Church the remission of our sins, and all other benefits of his passion.

And we pray that, by the presence and power of your Holy Spirit, all we who are partakers of this holy Communion may be filled with your grace and heavenly benediction; through Jesus Christ our Lord, by whom and with whom, in the unity of the Holy Spirit, all honor and glory be given to you, Father Almighty, forever and ever. *Amen.*

After a short period of silence the Priest says:

The peace of the Lord be always with you.
People: And with your spirit.

Holy Communion

Then the Priest, kneeling down at the Lord's Table, says with all who intend to receive the Holy Communion, this Prayer.

WE do not presume to come to this your table, merciful Lord, trusting in our own righteousness, but in your abundant and great mercies. We are not worthy so much as to gather up the crumbs under your table. But you are the same Lord, who always delights in showing mercy. Grant us, therefore, gracious Lord, so to eat the flesh of your dear Son Jesus Christ and to drink his blood, that our sinful bodies may be made clean by his body, and our souls washed through his most precious blood, and that we may evermore dwell in him, and he in us. Amen.

The Minister receives Communion and then delivers the same to the clergy and lay assistants. This done, the congregation comes forward in an orderly manner to receive Holy Communion as they kneel. The following words of administration are used.

THE body of our Lord Jesus Christ which was given for you, preserve your body and soul to everlasting life. Take and eat this in remembrance that Christ died for you and feed on him in your heart by faith with thanksgiving.

THE blood of our Lord Jesus Christ, which was shed for you, preserve your body and soul to everlasting life. Drink this in remembrance that Christ's blood was shed for you and be thankful.

Holy Communion

What remains of the consecrated bread and wine and which is not required for the communion of the sick after the Service may be consumed reverently now or at the end of the service.

In the time for receiving Communion hymns, spiritual songs or anthems may be used, such as **Agnus Dei.**

When all have communicated the Priest says,

Let us pray:

Traditional

OUR Father who art in heaven, Hallowed be thy Name, Thy kingdom come, Thy will be done, on earth as it is in heaven. Give us this day our daily bread; And forgive us our trespasses, as we forgive them that trespass against us; And lead us not into temptation, but deliver us from evil. For thine is the kingdom, the power and the glory, forever and ever. Amen.

Contemporary

OUR Father in heaven, hallowed be your name. Your kingdom come, your will be done, on earth as in heaven. Give us today our daily bread. Forgive us our sins as we forgive those who sin against us. Lead us not into temptation but deliver us from evil. For yours is the kingdom, and the power, and the glory, forever and ever. Amen.

Then is said by the Minister alone, or with the people, the following Prayer:

ALMIGHTY and ever-living God, we heartily thank you that you graciously feed us, who have duly received these holy mysteries, with the spiritual food

Holy Communion

of the most precious Body and Blood of your Son, our Savior Jesus Christ. We also thank you that you have assured us in this sacrament of your favor and goodness towards us, and that we are true members of the mystical body of your Son, the blessed company of all faithful people, and are also heirs, through hope, of your eternal kingdom.

Here we offer and present to you, O Lord, ourselves, our souls and bodies, to be a reasonable, holy, and living sacrifice. Fill us all who share in this Holy Communion with your grace and heavenly benediction. And although we are unworthy, through our many sins, to offer to you any sacrifice, yet we pray that you will accept this, the duty and service we owe. Do not weigh our merits but pardon our offenses, through Jesus Christ our Lord; by whom and with whom, in the unity of the Holy Spirit, all honor and glory are yours, Father Almighty, forever and ever. Amen

This hymn of praise or another is now said or sung by all.

GLORY be to God on high, and on earth peace, good will towards men. We praise you, we bless you, we worship you, we glorify you, we give thanks to you for your great glory, O Lord God, heavenly King, God the Father Almighty.

O Lord, the only-begotten Son, Jesus Christ; O Lord God, Lamb of God, Son of the Father; you who take away the sin of the world, have mercy on us. You who take away the sin of the world, receive our prayer. You

Holy Communion

who sit at the right hand of God the Father, have mercy on us.

For you only are holy; you only are the Lord; you only, O Christ, with the Holy Spirit, are most high in the glory of God the Father. Amen.

The Minister concludes the service with the Blessing.

THE peace of God, which passes all understanding, keep your hearts and minds in the knowledge and love of God, and of his Son Jesus Christ our Lord: and the blessing of God Almighty, the Father, the Son and the Holy Spirit, be among you, and remain with you always. *Amen.*

For the ending of all three Orders

A recessional hymn may be sung, after which a concluding prayer, as below, may be used by the Minister.

ALMIGHTY Lord and everlasting God, graciously direct, sanctify, and govern, we pray, our hearts and bodies in the ways of your laws, and in the obeying of your commandments, that through your most mighty protection, everywhere and always, we may be preserved in body and soul; through our Lord and Savior, Jesus Christ. *Amen.*

ALMIGHTY God, grant, we pray, that the words, which we have heard with our ears, may through your grace be so grafted inwardly in our hearts, that they may cause to grow within us the fruit of good works, to the honor and praise of your name; through Jesus Christ our Lord. *Amen.*

The Collects and Eucharistic Lectionary

Introduction

The use of the Collect in the western Church is a very ancient practice. Though short, the Collect conformed to a general structure consisting of the following parts, not all of which are necessary for every Collect. (1) The invocation of God, usually with mention of one or more of his attributes, e.g., "Almighty God." (2) The basis upon which the petition is to be offered. This is present as a relative clause, in which aspects of the nature or revelation of God are recalled, and it is in the second person singular—e.g., "[You] who hate nothing that you have made..." (3) The petition, e.g., "Create and make in us new and contrite hearts." (4) The object or purpose of the petition, e.g., "...that we may obtain... perfect remission and forgiveness." (5) The pleading of Christ's merits or an ascription of praise.

The Epistle and Gospel constitute the original Eucharistic Lectionary of the first editions of The Book of Common Prayer (1549 & 1552). This has a long history going back to the patristic era. To it have been added a recommended Old Testament reading and a Psalm, and these are taken from the Lectionary for The Book of Common Prayer (1662) of the Church of England.

The Sunday Collect is said on the week-days following except where other Collects are appointed.

ADVENT

The First Sunday in Advent

ALMIGHTY God, give us grace to cast away the deeds of darkness and to put on the armor of light, now in the time of this mortal life, in which your Son came to us in great humility; that on the last day, when he shall come again in his glorious Majesty to judge the living and the dead, we may rise to the life immortal; through him who is alive and reigns with you and the Holy Spirit, one God, now and forever. *Amen.*

The O.T. Lesson: Micah 4:1–7 · *The Psalm*: 25:1–9
The Epistle: Romans 13:8–14 · *The Gospel*: Matthew 21:1–13
This Collect is to be repeated every day, after the other Collects in Advent, until Christmas Day.

The Second Sunday in Advent

BLESSED Lord, you who caused all Holy Scriptures to be written for our instruction: Help us so to hear them, to read, note, learn, and inwardly digest them that, by patience and comfort of your holy Word, we may embrace and forever hold fast the hope of everlasting life, which you have given us in our Savior Jesus Christ. *Amen.*

The O.T. Lesson: 2 Kings 22:8–10, 23:1–3 · *The Psalm:* 50:1–6
The Epistle: Romans 15:4–13 · *The Gospel:* Luke 21:25–33

The Third Sunday in Advent

LORD Jesus Christ, you who at your first coming sent your messenger to prepare the way before you: Grant that the ministers and stewards of your holy truth may in like manner so prepare and make ready the way, by turning the hearts of the disobedient to the wisdom of the just, that at your second coming to judge the world, we may be found an acceptable people in your sight;

The Collects and Eucharistic Lectionary

you who live and reign with the Father and the Holy Spirit, one God, now and forever. *Amen.*

The O.T. Lesson: Isaiah 35 · *The Psalm*: 80:1–7
The Epistle: 1 Corinthians 4:1–5 · *The Gospel*: Matthew 11:2–10

The Fourth Sunday in Advent

Visit us, O Lord, we pray, with your power, and with great might come to our aid, because through our sins and wickedness we are severely hindered in running the race that is set before us; may your bountiful grace and mercy speedily help and deliver us; through Jesus Christ our Lord, to whom, with you and the Holy Spirit, be honor and glory, now and forever. *Amen.*

The O.T. Lesson: Isaiah 40:1–9 · *The Psalm*: 145:17–end.
The Epistle: Philippians 4:4–7 · *The Gospel*: John 1:19–28

THE CHRISTMAS SEASON

The Nativity of our Lord, or the Birthday of Christ, commonly called Christmas Day, December 25

Almighty God, you who have given us your only-begotten Son to take our nature upon him, and to be born of a pure Virgin: Grant that we, who have been born again and made your children by adoption and grace, may daily be renewed by your Holy Spirit; through Jesus Christ our Lord, who lives and reigns with you and the Holy Spirit, one God, now and forever. *Amen.*

The O.T. Lesson: Isaiah 9:2–7 · *The Psalm:* 98
The Epistle: Hebrews 1:1–12 · *The Gospel:* John 1:1–14
This Collect is to be used daily until the Eve of the Epiphany.

The Collects and Eucharistic Lectionary

Saint Stephen the Martyr (December 26)

GRANT, Lord Jesus Christ, that in all our sufferings here on earth, for the testimony of your truth, we may look up steadfastly to heaven and by faith behold the glory that shall be revealed; and also grant that being filled with the Holy Spirit, we may learn to love and bless our persecutors, as Stephen your first martyr prayed for his persecutors to you, blessed Jesus, who stand at the right hand of God to sustain all those who suffer for you, our only Mediator and Advocate. *Amen.*

The O.T. Lesson: 2 Chronicles 24:20–22 · *The Psalm:* 119:161–168
For the Epistle: Acts 7:55–60 · *The Gospel:* Matthew 23:34–39

Saint John the Evangelist (December 27)

MERCIFUL Lord, let the bright beams of your light shine upon your Church, we pray, so that, being enlightened by the teaching of your blessed apostle and evangelist Saint John, it may walk in the light of your truth, and come at the last to the light of everlasting life; through Jesus Christ our Lord. *Amen.*

The O.T. Lesson: Exodus 33:18–end · *The Psalm:* 92:11–end
The Epistle: 1 John 1:1–10 · *The Gospel:* John 21:19b–25

The Innocents (December 28)

ALMIGHTY God, you who have established praise out of the mouths of infants, and have made children by their deaths glorify you: Put to death all evil within us, and so strengthen us by your grace, that by the purity of our lives and constancy of our faith, we

The Collects and Eucharistic Lectionary

may glorify your holy Name; through Jesus Christ our Lord. *Amen.*

The O.T. Lesson: Jeremiah 31:10–17 · *The Psalm:* 123
The Epistle: Revelation 14:1–5 · *The Gospel:* Matthew 2:13–18

The First Sunday after Christmas Day

ALMIGHTY God, you who have given us your only-begotten Son to take our nature upon him, and to be born of a pure Virgin: Grant that we, who have been born again and made your children by adoption and grace, may daily be renewed by your Holy Spirit; through Jesus Christ our Lord, who lives and reigns with you and the Holy Spirit, one God, now and forever. *Amen.*

The O.T. Lesson: Isaiah 62:10–12 · *The Psalm:* 45:1–7
The Epistle: Galatians 4:1–7 · *The Gospel:* Matthew 1:18–25

The Second Sunday after Christmas

This Collect, Epistle and Gospel may be used on any day after the Circumcision and until the Epiphany.

ALMIGHTY God, you who wonderfully created man in your image, and yet more wonderfully restored him: Grant, we pray, that as your Son our Lord Jesus Christ was made in the likeness of men, so we may be made partakers of the divine nature; through the same your Son; who with you and the Holy Spirit lives and reigns one God, forever and ever. *Amen.*

The O.T. Lesson: Micah 4:1–5 & 5:2–4 · *The Psalm:* 110:1–4
The Epistle: 2 Corinthians 8:9 · *The Gospel:* John 1:14–18

The Collects and Eucharistic Lectionary

EPIPHANY SEASON

The Epiphany, or the Manifestation of Christ to the Gentiles (January 6)

Lord God, you who by the leading of a star revealed your Son to the Gentiles: Mercifully grant that we, who know you now by faith, may after this life behold your glory in the face of the same your Son, Jesus Christ our Lord. *Amen.*

> *The O.T. Lesson:* Isaiah 60:1–9 · *The Psalm:* 100
> *The Epistle:* Ephesians 3:1–12 · *The Gospel:* Matthew 2:1–12
> This Collect, Epistle and Gospel may be said on the seven days following except on the Sunday.
>
> The following Collect, Lesson and Gospel may be used on any weekday of the Octave or at a second service on the Epiphany.

The Baptism of our Lord

Father in heaven, whose blessed Son took our nature upon him, and was baptized for our sake in the river Jordan: Mercifully grant that we, being born anew, and made your children by adoption and grace, may also be partakers of your Holy Spirit; through him whom you sent to be our Savior and Redeemer, even the same your Son, Jesus Christ our Lord. *Amen.*

> *The O.T. Lesson:* Isaiah 42:1–8 · *The Psalm:* 29
> *For the Epistle:* Acts 10:34–43 · *The Gospel:* Mark 1:1–12

The First Sunday after the Epiphany

Lord God, we ask you mercifully to receive the prayers of your people who call upon you; and grant that they may both perceive and know what things they ought to do, and also may have grace and power faith-

fully to perform them; through Jesus Christ our Lord. *Amen*.
> *The O.T. Lesson*: Zechariah 8:1–8 · *The Psalm:* 72:1–8
> *The Epistle:* Romans 12:1–5 · *The Gospel*: Luke 2:41–52

The Second Sunday after the Epiphany

ALMIGHTY and everlasting God, you who rule over all things in heaven and earth: Mercifully hear the prayers of your people, and grant us your peace all the days of our life; through Jesus Christ our Lord. *Amen*.
> *The O.T. Lesson*: 2 Kgs 4:1–17 · *The Psalm*: 107:13–22
> *The Epistle*: Romans 12:6–15 · *The Gospel*: John 2:1–11

The Third Sunday after the Epiphany

ALMIGHTY and everlasting God, mercifully look upon our weaknesses and, in all dangers and needs, stretch out your right hand to help and defend us; through Jesus Christ our Lord. *Amen*.
> *The O.T. Lesson*: 2 Kgs 6:14b–23 · *The Psalm*: 102:15–22
> *The Epistle:* Romans 12:16–21 · *The Gospel:* Matthew 8:1–13

The Fourth Sunday after the Epiphany

LORD God, you who know that we are placed in the midst of so many and so great dangers, and that because of our human weakness we cannot always stand upright: Grant us such a measure of strength and protection that we may be supported in all dangers, and be carried through all temptations; through Jesus Christ our Lord. *Amen*.
> *The O.T. Lesson*: 1 Samuel 10:17–24 *The Psalm*: 97
> *The Epistle*: Romans 13:1–7 · *The Gospel*: Matthew 8:23–34

The Collects and Eucharistic Lectionary

The Fifth Sunday after the Epiphany

Lord God, we ask you to keep your household, the Church, continually in your true faith and devotion; so that they, who rely only upon the hope of your heavenly grace, may always be defended by your mighty power; through Jesus Christ our Lord. *Amen.*

The O.T. Lesson: Hosea 6:4–6 · *The Psalm*: 118:14–21
The Epistle: Colossians 3:12–17 · *The Gospel*: Matthew 13:24–30

The Sixth Sunday after the Epiphany

Lord God, whose blessed Son came to earth that he might destroy the works of the devil, and make us children of God and heirs of eternal life: Grant that we, who have this hope, may purify ourselves as he is pure, so that, when he shall come again in power and great glory, we may be made like him in his eternal and glorious kingdom; where with you, Father, and you, Holy Spirit, he lives and reigns, one God, now and forever. *Amen.*

The O.T. Lesson: Isaiah 4:2–6 · *The Psalm*: 96
The Epistle: 1 John 3:1–8 · *The Gospel*: Matthew 24:23–31

PRE-LENTEN SEASON

The Third Sunday before Lent, known as Septuagesima

Lord God, we ask you favorably to hear the prayers of your people; that we, who are justly punished

The Collects and Eucharistic Lectionary

for our offenses against you, may be mercifully delivered by your goodness; through Jesus Christ our Savior, who lives and reigns with you and the Holy Spirit, one God, now and forever. *Amen.*

The O.T. Lesson: Genesis 1:1–5 · *The Psalm:* 9:10–20
The Epistle: 1 Corinthians 9:24–27 · *The Gospel:* Matthew 20:1–16

The Second Sunday before Lent, known as Sexagesima

Lord God, you who see that we do not put our trust in any thing that we do: Mercifully grant that by your power we may be defended against all adversity; through Jesus Christ our Lord. *Amen.*

The O.T. Lesson: Genesis 3:9–19 · *The Psalm:* 83:1–2 & 13–end
The Epistle: 2 Corinthians 11:19–31 · *The Gospel:* Luke 8:4–15

The Sunday next before Lent, known as Quinquagesima

Lord God, you who have taught us that whatever we do without genuine love is worth nothing in your sight: Send your Holy Spirit and pour into our hearts this most excellent gift of love, the true bond of peace and of all virtues; for without such love whoever lives is reckoned as dead before you: Grant this for the sake of your only Son, Jesus Christ. *Amen.*

The O.T. Lesson: Genesis 9:8–17 · *The Psalm:* 77:11–end
The Epistle: 1 Corinthians 13:1–13 · *The Gospel:* Luke 18:31–43

The Collects and Eucharistic Lectionary

LENTEN SEASON

The First Day of Lent, commonly called Ash Wednesday

ALMIGHTY and eternal God, you who hate nothing that you have made, and who forgive the sins of all those who are penitent: Create and make in us new and contrite hearts, that we, worthily lamenting our sins and acknowledging our wretchedness, may obtain of you, the God of all mercy, perfect remission and forgiveness; through Jesus Christ our Lord. *Amen.*

The O.T. Lesson: Joel 2:12–17 · *The Psalm:* 57
The Epistle: James 4:1–10 · *The Gospel*: Matthew 6:16–21

This Collect is to be repeated, daily after the other Collects, throughout Lent until the Thursday before Easter inclusive.

The First Sunday in Lent

LORD Jesus Christ, you who for our sake fasted forty days and forty nights: Give us grace to use such abstinence, that, our flesh being subdued to the Spirit, we may always obey your godly discipline in righteousness and true holiness, to the honor and glory of your Name; who live and reign with the Father and the Holy Spirit, one God, now and forever. *Amen.*

The O.T. Lesson: Genesis 3:1–6 · *The Psalm:* 91:1–12
The Epistle: 2 Corinthians 6:1–10 · *The Gospel*: Matthew 4:1–11

The Second Sunday in Lent

ALMIGHTY God, you who see that we have no power of ourselves to help ourselves: Keep us both outwardly in our bodies and inwardly in our souls, so that

The Collects and Eucharistic Lectionary

we may be defended from all adversities which may happen to the body, and from all evil thoughts which may assault and hurt the soul; through Jesus Christ our Lord. *Amen.*

The O.T. Lesson: Jeremiah 17:5–10 · *The Psalm:* 25:13–end
The Epistle: 1 Thessalonians 4:1–8 · *The Gospel:* Matthew 15:21–28

The Third Sunday in Lent

ALMIGHTY God, consider the sincere desires of your humble servants, we humbly pray, and stretch out the right hand of your power to defend us against all our enemies; through Jesus Christ our Lord. *Amen.*

The O.T. Lesson: Numbers 22:21–31 · *The Psalm:* 9:13–end
The Epistle: Ephesians 5:1–14 · *The Gospel*: Luke 11:14–28

The Fourth Sunday in Lent

ALMIGHTY God, grant, we humbly pray, that we, who deserve to be punished for our evil deeds, may by your grace and mercy be spared; through Jesus Christ our Lord. *Amen.*

The O.T. Lesson: Exodus 16:2–7a · *The Psalm*: 122
The Epistle: Galatians 4:21 – 5:1 · *The Gospel*: John 6:1–14

The Fifth Sunday in Lent, commonly called Passion Sunday

ALMIGHTY God, look mercifully, we humbly pray, upon your people, so that, by your great goodness, we may be always governed and preserved both in body and soul; through Jesus Christ our Lord. *Amen.*

The O.T. Lesson: Exodus 24:4–8 · *The Psalm:* 143
The Epistle: Hebrews 9:11–15 · *The Gospel:* John 8:46–59

The Collects and Eucharistic Lectionary

The Sunday next before Easter, commonly called Palm Sunday

ALMIGHTY and eternal God, you who of your tender love towards the human race sent your Son, our Savior Jesus Christ, to take our human nature and flesh upon himself, and to suffer death upon the Cross, that we all should follow the example of his great humility: In your mercy grant that we may both follow the example of his patience, and also be made partakers of his resurrection; through Jesus Christ our Lord. *Amen.*

The O.T. Lesson: Zechariah 9:9–12 · *The Psalm:* 73:22–end
The Epistle: Philippians 2:5–11 · *The Gospel:* Matthew 27:1–54
This Collect shall be used until Maundy Thursday inclusive.

Monday in Holy Week

The O.T. Lesson: Isaiah 63:1–19 · *The Psalm:* 55:1–8
The Epistle: Galatians 6:1–11 · *The Gospel:* Mark 14:1–72

Tuesday in Holy Week

The O.T. Lesson: Isaiah 50:5–11 · *The Psalm:* 13
The Epistle: Romans 5:6–19 · *The Gospel:* Mark 15:1–39

Wednesday in Holy Week

The O.T. Lesson: Isaiah 49:1–9a · *The Psalm:* 54
The Epistle: Hebrews 9:16–28 · *The Gospel:* Luke 22:1–71

Thursday before Easter, commonly called Maundy Thursday

LORD Jesus Christ, you who in this wonderful Sacrament have given us a memorial of your passion: Grant us so to reverence the sacred mysteries of your

The Collects and Eucharistic Lectionary

body and blood, that we may know within ourselves the fruits of your redemption; who are alive and reign with the Father and the Holy Spirit, one God, now and forever. *Amen.*

The O.T. Lesson: Exodus 12:1–11 · *The Psalm*: 43
The Epistle: 1 Corinthians 11:17–34 · *The Gospel*: Luke 23:1–49

Good Friday

Almighty God, we pray you graciously to look on this your family, for which our Lord Jesus Christ was willing to be betrayed and given up into the hands of sinners, and to suffer death upon the Cross; who lives and reigns with you and the Holy Spirit, one God, now and forever. *Amen.*

Almighty and everlasting God, by whose Spirit the whole body of the Church is governed and sanctified: Receive our petitions and prayers which we offer to you for the various members of your holy Church, so that in their vocation and ministry they may truly and devoutly serve you; through Jesus Christ our Lord. *Amen.*

Merciful Father, you who have made all peoples, and neither hate anything that you have made nor desire the death of sinners, but rather intend that they should be converted and live: Have mercy upon all who do not know you as you are revealed in the Gospel of your Son. Take from them all ignorance, hardness of heart, and contempt for your Word, and bring them home to your sheepfold, blessed Lord, so that they may

The Collects and Eucharistic Lectionary

all become one flock under one shepherd, Jesus Christ our Lord, who lives and reigns with you and the Holy Spirit, one God, now and forever. *Amen.*

The O.T. Lesson: Numbers 21:4–9 · *The Psalm:* 140:1–9
The Epistle: Hebrews 10:1–25 · *The Gospel:* John 19:1–37

Easter Eve or Holy Saturday

GRANT, Father, that we, who have been baptized into the death of your blessed Son, our Savior Jesus Christ, may continually put to death our evil desires and be buried with him; so that we may pass through the grave, the gate of death, to our joyful resurrection through his merits who died, was buried, and rose again for us, your Son, Jesus Christ our Lord. *Amen.*

The O.T. Lesson: Job 14:1–14 *The Psalm:* 142
The Epistle: 1 Peter 3:17–22 · *The Gospel:* Matthew 27:57–66

THE EASTER SEASON

Easter Day

These Anthems may be used at the Holy Communion at any suitable place in the Service before the Prayer for the Church.

The Easter Anthems—2 Corinthians 5:7-8; Romans 6:9–11; 1 Corinthians 15:20–22

CHRIST our Passover has been sacrificed for us: therefore let us celebrate the feast.

Not with the old leaven of corruption and wickedness; but with the unleavened bread of sincerity and truth.

The Collects and Eucharistic Lectionary

Christ, once raised from the dead dies no more; death has no more dominion over him. In dying, he died to sin once for all; in living, he lives to God. See yourselves therefore as dead to sin: and alive to God in Jesus Christ our Lord.

Christ has been raised from the dead: the first-fruits of those who sleep. For as by man came death: by man has come also the resurrection of the dead. For as in Adam all die: even so in Christ shall all be made alive.

Glory be to the Father, and to the Son, and to the Holy Spirit: as it was in the beginning, is now, and shall be forever; world without end. Amen.

A LMIGHTY Father and ever-living God, you who through your only-begotten Son Jesus Christ have overcome death, and opened to us the gate of eternal life: We humbly pray that, through your grace going before us, good desires will enter into our minds, and, by your continual help, we shall be enabled to bring them to right fulfillment; through Jesus Christ our Lord, who lives and reigns with you and the Holy Spirit, one God, now and forever. *Amen.*

The O.T. Lesson: Exodus 12:21–28 · *The Psalm*: 111
The Epistle: Colossians 3:1–7 · *The Gospel*: John 20:1–10
This Collect is to be said throughout Easter Week.

The following Collect may be used as an additional Collect on Easter Day and seven days following.

GRACIOUS God, you who make us glad with the yearly remembering of the resurrection from the

The Collects and Eucharistic Lectionary

dead of your only Son Jesus Christ: Grant that we who celebrate this Paschal feast may die daily unto sin, and live with him forever in the glory of his endless life; through the same Jesus Christ our Lord. *Amen*

Monday in Easter Week
The O.T. Lesson: Hosea 6:1–6 *For the Psalm*: Easter Anthems
The Epistle: Acts 10:34–43 · *The Gospel*: Luke 24:13–35

Tuesday in Easter Week
The O.T. Lesson: 1 Kings 17:17–end · *The Psalm*: 16:9–end
The Epistle: Acts 13:26–41 · *The Gospel*: Luke 24:36–48

The First Sunday after Easter, commonly called Low Sunday

ALMIGHTY Father, you who gave your only Son to die for our sins, and to rise again for our justification: Grant that we may put away the old yeast of malice and wickedness in order always to serve you in sincerity and truth; through the merits of your Son, Jesus Christ our Lord. *Amen*.

The O.T. Lesson: Ezekiel 37:1–10 · *The Psalm*: 81:1–4
The Epistle: 1 John 5:4–12 · *The Gospel*: John 20:19–23

The Second Sunday after Easter

ALMIGHTY Father, you who have given your only Son to be for us both a sacrifice for sin and also an example of godly life: Give us grace that we may always receive with thankfulness the immeasurable benefit of his sacrifice, and also try daily to follow in the blessed steps of his most holy life; through Jesus Christ our Lord. *Amen.*

The O.T. Lesson: Ezekiel 34:11–16a · *The Psalm*: 23
The Epistle: 1 Peter 2:19–25 · *The Gospel*: John 10:11–16

The Third Sunday after Easter

ALMIGHTY God, you who show the light of your truth to those in error, so that they may return into the way of righteousness: Grant to all who are admitted into the fellowship of Christ's religion, that they may shun everything that is contrary to their profession, and follow whatever is in agreement with it; through our Lord Jesus Christ. *Amen.*

The O.T. Lesson: Genesis 45:3–10 · *The Psalm*: 57
The Epistle: 1 Peter 2:11–17 · *The Gospel*: John 16:16–22

The Fourth Sunday after Easter

ALMIGHTY God, you who alone can order the unruly wills and emotions of sinful people: Grant unto your elect people, that they may love the thing which you command, and desire that which you promise; so that among the many and varied changes of the world, our hearts may firmly be established where true joys are to be found; through Jesus Christ our Lord. *Amen.*

The O.T. Lesson: Job 19:21–27a · *The Psalm*: 57
The Epistle: James 1:17–21 · *The Gospel*: John 16:5–15

The Fifth Sunday after Easter, commonly called Rogation Sunday

LORD God, from whom all good things come: Grant to us your humble servants that, by your holy inspi-

The Collects and Eucharistic Lectionary

ration, we may think those things that are good, and, by your merciful guidance, may put them into practice; through our Lord Jesus Christ. *Amen.*

The O.T. Lesson: Joel 2:21–26 · *The Psalm*: 66:1–8
The Epistle: James 1:22–27 · *The Gospel*: John 16:23–33

THE SEASON OF ASCENSION

The Ascension Day, being the Fortieth Day after Easter

ALMIGHTY Father and ever-living God, we truly believe that your only-begotten Son our Lord Jesus Christ has ascended into heaven: Grant, we pray, that we may also in heart and mind ascend there, and continually dwell with him; who lives and reigns with you and the Holy Spirit, one God, now and forever. *Amen.*

The O.T. Lesson: Daniel 7:13–14 · *The Psalm*: 68:1–6
For the Epistle: Acts 1:1–11 · *The Gospel:* Mark 16:14–20 or
Luke 24:44–53

The Collect, Epistle and Gospel are used on the seven days following, except when other provision is made.

The Sunday after Ascension Day

FATHER Almighty, the King of glory, you who exalted your only Son Jesus Christ with great triumph to your kingdom in heaven: We desire that you do not to leave us desolate, but pray that you will send your Spirit to strengthen us, and to exalt us to the place to which our Savior has already gone; who lives and reigns with you and the Holy Spirit, one God now and forever. *Amen.*

The Collects and Eucharistic Lectionary

The O.T. Lesson: 2 Kings 2:9–15 · *The Psalm*: 68:32–end
The Epistle: 1 Peter 4:7–11 · *The Gospel*: John 15:26 – 16:4

WHITSUNTIDE
Whitsunday, also known as Pentecost

> These Anthems may be used at the Holy Communion at any suitable place in the Service before the Prayer for the Church.

The Whitsuntide Anthems—Psalm 98:1; Acts 2:33; Galatians 4:6; 2 Corinthians 3:18

SING to the Lord a new song, for he has done marvelous things.

Being therefore exalted at the right hand of God, and having received from the Father the promise of the Holy Spirit, he has poured out this that you yourselves are seeing and hearing.

And because you are sons, God has sent the Spirit of his Son into our hearts, crying, "Abba, Father."

We all, with unveiled face, beholding the glory of the Lord, are being transformed into the same image from one degree of glory to another.

Glory be to the Father and to the Son and to the Holy Spirit: as it was in the beginning, is now, and shall be forever; world without end. Amen.

ALMIGHTY God, you who taught the hearts of your faithful people by sending to them the light of your Holy Spirit: Grant that by the same Spirit we may judge all things rightly and always rejoice in his holy strengthening and protection; through the merits of

The Collects and Eucharistic Lectionary

Christ Jesus our Savior, who lives and reigns with you and the Holy Spirit, one God, now and forever. *Amen*.

This shall be used for six days following until the Eve of Trinity Sunday.

The following additional Collect may also be used.

GRACIOUS God, you who make us glad with the yearly remembering of the coming of the Holy Spirit upon your disciples in Jerusalem: Grant that we, who celebrate before you the Feast of Pentecost, may continue yours forever, and daily increase in your Holy Spirit, until we come to your eternal kingdom; through Jesus Christ our Lord. *Amen*.

The O.T. Lesson: Deuteronomy 16:9–12 · *The Psalm*: 122
The Epistle: Acts 2:1–11 · *The Gospel*: John 14:15–31a

Monday in Whitsun Week

The O.T. Lesson: Numbers 11:24–30
For the Psalm: Whitsuntide Anthems
The Epistle: Acts 10:34–48 · *The Gospel*: John 3:16–21

Tuesday in Whitsun Week

The O.T. Lesson: Ezekiel 37:1–14
For the Psalm: Whitsuntide Anthems
The Epistle: Acts 8:14–17 *The Gospel*: John 10:1–10

TRINITY SEASON

Trinity Sunday

ALMIGHTY and everlasting God, by whose gift your servants, in confessing the true Faith, acknowledge the glory of the eternal Trinity and adore the Unity in the power of your Majesty: Grant that by steadfastness of the same Faith, we may always be defended from all adversities; through our Lord Jesus Christ, your Son, who lives and reigns, with you, in the unity of the Holy Spirit, one God, now and forever. *Amen.*

The O.T. Lesson: Isaiah 6:1–8 · *The Psalm*: 8
The Epistle: Revelation 4: 1–11 · *The Gospel*: John 3:1–15

The First Sunday after Trinity

Lord God, the strength of all who put their trust in you, mercifully accept our prayers; and, because through the weakness of our human nature we cannot do anything good without you, grant us the help of your grace, so that in keeping your commandments we may please you both in will and deed; through Jesus Christ our Lord. *Amen.*

The O.T. Lesson: 2 Samuel 9:6–end · *The Psalm*: 41:1–4
The Epistle: 1 John 4:7–21 · *The Gospel*: Luke 16:19–31

The Second Sunday after Trinity

Lord God, the unfailing helper and guide of those whom you nurture in your steadfast fear and love: Keep us, we pray, under the protection of your good providence, and give us a continual reverence and love for your holy Name; through Jesus Christ our Lord. *Amen.*

The O.T. Lesson: Genesis 12:1–4 · *The Psalm:* 120
The Epistle: 1 John 3:13–end · *The Gospel*: Luke 14:16–24

The Third Sunday after Trinity

Lord God, mercifully hear us, we humbly pray, and grant that we, to whom you have given a sincere

The Collects and Eucharistic Lectionary

desire to pray, may be defended by your mighty power, and strengthened in all dangers and adversities; through Jesus Christ our Lord. *Amen.*

The O.T. Lesson: 2 Chronicles 33:9–13 · *The Psalm:* 55:17–23
The Epistle: 1 Peter 5:5–11 · *The Gospel:* Luke 15:1–10

The Fourth Sunday after Trinity

Lord God, the protector of all who trust in you, and without whom nothing is strong or holy: Increase and multiply upon us your mercy, that with you as our ruler and guide, we may so pass through the things of this age, that finally we do not lose the things of the age to come: Grant this, heavenly Father, for our Lord Jesus Christ's sake. *Amen.*

The O.T. Lesson: Genesis 3:17–19 · *The Psalm:* 79:8–10
The Epistle: Romans 8:18–23 · *The Gospel:* Luke 6:36–42

The Fifth Sunday after Trinity

Lord God, we ask you so to govern the course of this world by your providence, that it may be peacefully ordered, and that your Church may joyfully serve you in all godly and quiet devotion; through Jesus Christ our Lord. *Amen.*

The O.T. Lesson: 1 Kings 19:19–21 · *The Psalm:* 84:8–end
The Epistle: 1 Peter 3:8–15a · *The Gospel:* Luke 5:1–11

The Sixth Sunday after Trinity

Lord God, you who have prepared for those who love you such good things that surpass our understanding: Pour into our hearts such love towards you that, loving you above all things, we may obtain your

The Collects and Eucharistic Lectionary

promises, which are greater than we can desire; through Jesus Christ our Lord. *Amen.*

The O.T. Lesson: Genesis 4:2b–15 · *The Psalm*: 90:12–end
The Epistle: Romans 6:3–11 · *The Gospel:* Matthew 5:20–26

The Seventh Sunday after Trinity

Lord of all power and might, the author and giver of all good things: Graft the love of your Name in our hearts, increase in us true piety and devotion, nourish us with all that is good, and by your great mercy keep us faithful; through Jesus Christ our Lord. *Amen.*

The O.T. Lesson: 1 Kings 17:8–16 · *The Psalm:* 34:11–end
The Epistle: Romans 6:19–23 · *The Gospel:* Mark 8:1–10a

The Eighth Sunday after Trinity

Lord God, whose never-failing providence governs everything in heaven and on earth: Take away from us all that is hurtful, we humbly pray, and give us that which is profitable for our salvation; through Jesus Christ our Lord. *Amen.*

The O.T. Lesson: Jeremiah 23:16–24 · *The Psalm*: 31:1–6
The Epistle: Romans 8:12–17 · *The Gospel*: Matthew 7:15–21

The Ninth Sunday after Trinity

Lord God, grant to us the spirit always to think and to do those things that are right, so that we, who cannot do anything good without you, may by your help be enabled to live according to your will; through Jesus Christ our Lord. *Amen.*

The O.T. Lesson: Numbers 10:35–11:3 · *The Psalm*: 95
The Epistle: 1 Corinthians 10:1–13 · *The Gospel:* Luke 16:1–9 or 15:11–31

The Collects and Eucharistic Lectionary

The Tenth Sunday after Trinity

Lord God, let your merciful ears be open to the prayers of your people and, in order that we may obtain our petitions, teach us to ask for those things that please you; through Jesus Christ our Lord. *Amen.*

The O.T. Lesson: Jeremiah 7:9–15 · *The Psalm*: 17:1–8
The Epistle: 1 Corinthians 12:1–11 · *The Gospel*: Luke 19:41–47a

The Eleventh Sunday after Trinity

Lord God, you who show your almighty power most of all in showing mercy and pity: Mercifully grant us such a measure of your grace, that in obeying your holy commandments we may obtain your gracious promises, and share in your heavenly treasure; through Jesus Christ our Lord. *Amen.*

The O.T. Lesson: 1 Kings 3:5–15 · *The Psalm:* 28
The Epistle: 1 Corinthians 15:1–11 · *The Gospel:* Luke 18:9–14

The Twelfth Sunday after Trinity

Almighty and everlasting God, you who are always more ready to hear than we are to pray, and who are willing to give more than either we desire or deserve: Pour down upon us the abundance of your mercy, forgiving us those things that cause guilt within us, and giving us those good things which we are not worthy to ask, except through the merits and mediation of Jesus Christ, your Son, our Lord. *Amen.*

The O.T. Lesson: Exodus 34:29–end · *The Psalm:* 34:1–10
The Epistle: 2 Corinthians 3:4–9 · *The Gospel:* Mark 7:31–37

The Collects and Eucharistic Lectionary

The Thirteenth Sunday after Trinity

ALMIGHTY and merciful God, by whose grace alone your faithful people offer you true and worthy service: Grant that we may so faithfully serve you in this life that we do not fail to obtain your heavenly promises in the life to come; through the merits of Jesus Christ our Lord. *Amen.*

The O.T. Lesson: Leviticus 19:13–18 · *The Psalm:* 74:20–end
The Epistle: Galatians 3:16–22 · *The Gospel*: Luke 10:23–37

The Fourteenth Sunday after Trinity

ALMIGHTY and everlasting God, grant that by your help we grow in faith, hope and love; and, so that we may obtain what you promise, make us also to love what you command; through Jesus Christ our Lord. *Amen.*

The O.T. Lesson: 2 Kings 5:9–16 · *The Psalm*: 118:1–9
The Epistle: Galatians 5:16–24 · *The Gospel*: Luke 17:11–19

The Fifteenth Sunday after Trinity

GUARD your Church, O Lord, with your perpetual mercy; and, because in our frailty we cannot stand without your support, keep us always from all that may harm us; and lead us to all that is profitable for our salvation; through Jesus Christ our Lord. *Amen.*

The O.T. Lesson: Joshua 24:14–25 · *The Psalm:* 92:1–6
The Epistle: Galatians 6:11–18 · *The Gospel*: Matthew 6:24–34

The Collects and Eucharistic Lectionary

The Sixteenth Sunday after Trinity

Lord God, let your continual pity cleanse and defend your Church, we humbly pray; and, because it cannot continue in safety without your aid, always preserve and protect it by your help and goodness; through Jesus Christ our Lord. *Amen.*

The O.T. Lesson: I Kings 17:17–end · *The Psalm*: 102:12–17
The Epistle: Ephesians 3:13–21 · *The Gospel*: Luke 7:11–17

The Seventeenth Sunday after Trinity

Lord God, we pray that your grace may always surround us, and that also you will make us to be continually committed to all good works; through Jesus Christ our Lord. *Amen.*

The O.T. Lesson: Proverbs 25:6–14 · *The Psalm:* 33:6–12
The Epistle: Ephesians 4:1–6 · *The Gospel*: Luke 14:1–11

The Eighteenth Sunday after Trinity

Lord God, give your people grace, we humbly pray, to withstand the temptations of the world, the flesh and the devil, and to follow you, the only true God, with pure hearts and minds; through Jesus Christ our Lord. *Amen.*

The O.T. Lesson: Deuteronomy 6:4–9 · *The Psalm:* 122
The Epistle: 1 Corinthians 1:4–8 · *The Gospel*: Matthew 22:34–46

The Nineteenth Sunday after Trinity

Lord God, without your help we are not able to please you; mercifully grant that your Holy Spirit

The Collects and Eucharistic Lectionary

may in all things direct and rule our hearts; through Jesus Christ our Lord. *Amen.*
> *The O.T. Lesson:* Genesis 18:23–32 · *The Psalm:* 141:1–9
> *The Epistle:* Ephesians 4:17–32 · *The Gospel:* Matthew 9:1–8

The Twentieth Sunday after Trinity

Almighty and most merciful God, keep us by your bountiful goodness, we pray you, from all things that may hurt us, so that we may be always ready both in body and soul cheerfully to accomplish whatever you would have us do; through Jesus Christ our Lord. *Amen.*
> *The O.T. Lesson:* Proverbs 9:1–6 · *The Psalm:* 145:15–end
> *The Epistle*: Ephesians 5:15–21 · *The Gospel:* Matthew 22:1–14

The Twenty-First Sunday after Trinity

Merciful Lord, grant, we humbly pray, to your faithful people pardon and peace, that they may be cleansed from all their sins and serve you with a quiet mind; through Jesus Christ our Lord. *Amen.*
> *The O.T. Lesson:* Genesis 32:24–29 · *The Psalm:* 90:1–12
> *The Epistle:* Ephesians 6:10–20 · *The Gospel:* John 4:46–54

The Twenty-Second Sunday after Trinity

Lord God, keep your household the Church grounded in continual godliness, we humbly pray, so that by your protection it may be free from all adversities, and may devoutly serve you in good works to the glory of your name; through Jesus Christ our Lord. *Amen.*
> *The O.T. Lesson:* Isaiah 11:1–10 · *The Psalm:* 44:1–9
> *The Epistle:* Philippians 1:3–11 · *The Gospel:* Matthew 18:21–35

The Collects and Eucharistic Lectionary

The Twenty-Third Sunday after Trinity

LORD God, our refuge and strength, and the author of all godliness: Be ready to hear the devout prayers of your Church, and grant that what we ask faithfully we may obtain effectually; through Jesus Christ our Lord. *Amen.*

The O.T. Lesson: Genesis 45:1–7,15 · *The Psalm:* 133
The Epistle: Philippians 3:17–21 · *The Gospel:* Matthew 22:15–22

The Twenty-Fourth Sunday after Trinity

LORD God, we humbly ask you to absolve your people from their offences against you; so that, through your bountiful goodness, we all may be set free from the chains of those sins, which in our frailty we have committed: Grant this, heavenly Father, for the sake of Jesus Christ, our blessed Lord and Savior. *Amen*

The O.T. Lesson: Isaiah 55:6–11 · *The Psalm*: 85:1–7
The Epistle: Colossians 1:3–12 · *The Gospel*: Matthew 9:18–26

The Sunday next before Advent

STIR up the wills of your faithful people, we pray you, O Lord, so that they may produce in abundance the fruit of good works, and then by you be abundantly rewarded; through Jesus Christ our Lord. *Amen.*

The O.T. Lesson: Jeremiah 23:5–8 · *The Psalm:* 85:8–end
The Epistle: Colossians 1:13–20 · *The Gospel:* John 6:5–14

The Collects and Eucharistic Lectionary

SAINTS' and other HOLY DAYS

Saint Andrew's Day (November 30)

ALMIGHTY God, you who gave such grace to your apostle Andrew that he readily obeyed the calling of your Son Jesus Christ, and followed him without delay: Grant that we, who are called by your holy Word, may also commit ourselves to obey your commandments; through the same Jesus Christ our Lord. *Amen.*

The O.T. Lesson: Isaiah 52:7–10 · *The Psalm*: 19:1–6
The Epistle: Romans 10:9–21 · *The Gospel*: Matthew 4:18–22

Saint Thomas the Apostle (December 21 or July 3)

ALMIGHTY and ever-living God, you who, for the firmer foundation of our faith, permitted your holy apostle Thomas to doubt your Son's resurrection until word and sight convinced him of it: Grant that we may perfectly, and without any doubt, believe in your Son Jesus Christ, so that our faith may never be found wanting in your sight; through the same Jesus Christ, to whom, with you and the Holy Spirit, be all honor and glory, now and forever. *Amen.*

The O.T. Lesson: Job 42:1–6 · *The Psalm:* 139::–1–11
The Epistle: Ephesians 2:19–end · *The Gospel:* John 20:24–31

The Circumcision of Christ (January 1)

ALMIGHTY God, you who caused your blessed Son to be circumcised and obedient to the law for all people: Grant us the true circumcision of the Spirit; that, all sinful desires in our hearts and bodies being put to death, we may obey your perfect will in all things; through your Son, Jesus Christ our Lord. *Amen.*

Eternal Lord God, you who have brought your servants to the beginning of another year: Pardon, we humbly pray, our transgressions in the past, and graciously abide with us all the days of our life; through Jesus Christ our Lord. *Amen.*

The O.T. Lesson: Genesis 17:3b–10 · *The Psalm*: 98
The Epistle: Rom.4:8–13 or Eph.2:11–18 · *The Gospel:* Luke 2:15–21

The Conversion of Saint Paul (January 25)

Lord God, you who, through the preaching of the blessed apostle Saint Paul, have caused the light of the Gospel to shine throughout the world: Grant, we pray, that, as we remember his wonderful conversion, we may show our thankfulness by following the holy doctrine which he taught; through Jesus Christ our Lord. *Amen.*

The O.T. Lesson: Joshua 5:13–end · *The Psalm:* 67
The Epistle: Acts 9:1–22 · *The Gospel*: Matthew 19:27–30

The Presentation of Christ in the Temple or The Purification of Saint Mary (February 2)

Almighty and ever-living God, we humbly pray that, as your only Son was presented this day in the temple in our human nature and flesh, so may we be presented to you with pure and clean hearts by the same your Son Jesus Christ our Lord. *Amen.*

The O.T. Lesson: Malachi 3:1–5 · *The Psalm:* 48:1–7
For the Epistle: Galatians 4:1–7 · *The Gospel:* Luke 2:22–40

The Collects and Eucharistic Lectionary

Saint Matthias the Apostle (February 24 or May 14)

ALMIGHTY God, you who chose your faithful servant Matthias to be numbered among the twelve apostles in place of the traitor Judas: Grant that your Church may always be preserved from false apostles, and ordered and guided by faithful and true pastors; through Jesus Christ our Lord. *Amen.*

The O.T. Lesson: 1 Samuel 2:27–35 · *The Psalm:* 16:1–7
The Epistle: Acts 1:15–26 · *The Gospel:* Matthew 11:25–30

The Annunciation of the Blessed Virgin Mary (March 25)

LORD God, pour your grace into our hearts, we pray, that as we have known the incarnation of your Son Jesus Christ by the message of an angel, so by his cross and passion we may be brought to the glory of his resurrection; through the same Jesus Christ our Lord. *Amen.*

The O.T. Lesson: Isaiah 7:10–15 · *The Psalm:* 113
The Epistle: Romans 5:12–19 · *The Gospel:* Luke 1:26–38

Saint Mark the Evangelist (April 25)

ALMIGHTY God, you who have instructed your holy Church through the inspired teaching of your Evangelist Saint Mark: Give us grace so that we may not be carried away with every wind of false teaching, but may rather be established in the truth of your holy Gospel; through Jesus Christ our Lord. *Amen.*

The O.T. Lesson: Proverbs 15:28–end · *The Psalm:* 119:9–16
The Epistle: Ephesians 4:7–16 · *The Gospel*: John 15:1–11

The Collects and Eucharistic Lectionary

Saint Philip and Saint James the Apostles (May 1)

ALMIGHTY God, whom truly to know is everlasting life: Teach us perfectly to know your Son Jesus Christ as the way, the truth, and the life, that we may follow in the steps of your holy apostles Philip and James, and walk steadfastly in the way that leads to eternal life; through the same your Son, Jesus Christ our Lord. *Amen.*

The O.T. Lesson: Proverbs 4:10–18 · *The Psalm:* 25:1–9
The Epistle: James 1:1–12 · *The Gospel:* John 14:1–14

Saint Barnabas the Apostle (June 11)

LORD God almighty, you who endowed your holy apostle Barnabas with special gifts of the Holy Spirit so that he could effectively encourage others: Do not leave us, we pray, destitute of your gifts, or of the grace always to use them for your honor and glory; through Jesus Christ our Lord. *Amen.*

The O.T. Lesson: Job 29:11–16 · *The Psalm:* 112
The Epistle: Acts 11:22–30 · *The Gospel:* John 15:12–16

Saint John the Baptist (June 24)

ALMIGHTY God, by whose providence your servant John the Baptist was wonderfully born and sent to prepare the way for your Son our Savior, by the preaching of repentance: Make us so to follow his teaching and holy life, that we may truly repent, constantly speak the truth, boldly rebuke vice, and patiently suffer for the truth's sake; through Jesus Christ our Lord. *Amen.*

The O.T. Lesson: Isaiah 40:1–11 · *The Psalm:* 80:1–7
For the Epistle: Acts 13:22–26 · *The Gospel:* Luke 1:57–80

The Collects and Eucharistic Lectionary

Saint Peter or Saint Peter and Saint Paul (June 29)

ALMIGHTY God, you who by your Son Jesus Christ gave to your Apostle Saint Peter many excellent gifts and commanded him earnestly to feed your flock: Make, we humbly pray, all bishops and pastors diligently to preach your holy Word and the people obediently to follow the same, that they may receive the crown of everlasting glory; through Jesus Christ our Lord. *Amen.*

The O.T. Lesson: Ezekiel 3:4–11 · *The Psalm:* 125
The Epistle: Acts 12:1–11 · *The Gospel:* Matthew 16: 13–19

When June 29 is kept as a joint festival for both Saint Peter and Saint Paul then the Epistle and the Gospel remain the same but the Collect is as follows:

ALMIGHTY God, whose blessed apostles Peter and Paul glorified you in their death as in their life: Grant that your Church, inspired by their teaching and example, and made one by your Spirit, may ever stand firm upon the one foundation, Jesus Christ your Son our Lord; who is alive and reigns with you in the unity of the Holy Spirit, one God, now and forever. *Amen.*

Saint Mary Magdalene (July 22)

ALMIGHTY God, whose beloved Son restored Mary Magdalene to health of mind and body and called her to be a witness to his resurrection: Mercifully grant that by your grace we may be healed in body and soul, and always serve you in the power of his risen life; who is alive and reigns with you in the unity of the Holy Spirit, one God, now and forever. *Amen.*

The Collects and Eucharistic Lectionary

The O.T. Lesson: Zephaniah 3:14–end · *The Psalm:* Psalm 30:1–5
The Epistle: 2 Corinthians 5:14–17 · *The Gospel:* John 20:11–18

Saint James the Apostle (July 25)

MERCIFUL Lord, whose holy apostle Saint James left his father and mother and all that he had, to be obedient to the calling of your Son Jesus Christ, and followed him even unto death: Grant that we may always be ready to forsake all false attractions and pleasures of this world, and of the flesh, and to follow your holy commandments; through Jesus Christ our Lord. *Amen*.

The O.T. Lesson: 2 Kings 1:9–15 · *The Psalm:* 15
The Epistle: Acts 11:27–12:3a · *The Gospel:* Matthew 20:20–28

The Transfiguration of our Lord (August 6)

HEAVENLY Father, you who before the passion of your only Son revealed his true glory upon the holy mountain to chosen witnesses: Grant that beholding the light of his transfigured face by faith, we, your servants, may be strengthened to bear the cross, and be changed into his likeness from glory to glory; through Jesus Christ our Lord. *Amen*.

The O.T. Lesson: Exodus 24:12–end · *The Psalm:* 84:1–7
The Epistle: 1 John 3:1–3 · *The Gospel*: Mark 9:2–7

Saint Bartholomew the Apostle (August 24)

ALMIGHTY and everlasting God, you who gave to your apostle Bartholomew grace truly to believe and preach your Word: Grant, we humbly pray, that your Church may love the word which he believed, and may faithfully preach and receive the same; through Jesus Christ our Lord. *Amen.*

The O.T. Lesson: Genesis 28:10–17 · *The Psalm:* 15
The Epistle: Acts 5: 12–16 · *The Gospel:* Luke 22:24–30

Saint Matthew the Apostle (September 21)

ALMIGHTY God, you who by your beloved Son called Matthew the tax-collector to be an Apostle and Evangelist: Give us grace to forsake all covetous desires and the possessive love of riches, so that we may follow your Son Jesus Christ; who is alive and reigns with you, in the unity of the Holy Spirit, one God, now and forever. *Amen.*

The O.T. Lesson: Isaiah 33:13–17 · *The Psalm:* 119:65–72
The Epistle: 2 Corinthians 4:1–6 · *The Gospel:* Matthew 9:9–13

Saint Michael and All Angels (September 29)

EVERLASTING God, by whom the ministries of angels and humans have been ordained and constituted in a wonderful order: Mercifully grant that, as your holy angels always serve you in heaven, so by your command they may help and defend us here on earth; through Jesus Christ our Lord. *Amen.*

The O.T. Lesson: Daniel 10:10–19a · *The Psalm:* 103:17–22
The Epistle: Revelation 12:7–12 · *The Gospel:* Matthew 18:1–10

Saint Luke the Evangelist (October 18)

ALMIGHTY God, you who called Luke the physician to be an evangelist and physician of the soul, and under your guidance wrote the Gospel bearing his name: Grant that, by the wholesome medicines of teaching written by him, all the diseases of our souls may be healed; through the merits of Jesus Christ our Lord. *Amen.*

The O.T. Lesson: Isaiah 35:3–6 · *The Psalm*: 147:1–6
The Epistle: 2 Timothy 4:5–15 · *The Gospel:* Luke 10:1–9 or 7:36–50

Saint Simon and Saint Jude, Apostles (October 28)

ALMIGHTY God, you who built your Church on the foundation of the apostles and prophets, with Jesus Christ himself as the chief corner-stone: Grant us so to be joined together in unity of spirit by their teaching, that we may be made a holy temple acceptable to you; through Jesus Christ our Lord. *Amen.*

The O.T. Lesson: Isaiah 28:9–16 · *The Psalm*: 116:11–end
The Epistle: Jude 1–8 or Rev.21:9–14 · *The Gospel*: John 15: 17–27

All Saints' Day (November 1)

ALMIGHTY God, you who have joined together your elect in one communion and fellowship in the mystical body of your Son Christ our Lord: Grant us grace so to follow your blessed saints in all virtuous and godly living, that we may come to those inexpressible joys that you have prepared for those who truly love you; through Jesus Christ our Lord. *Amen.*

The O.T. Lesson: Isaiah 66:20–23 · *The Psalm*: 33:1–5
The Epistle: Revelation 7:2–12 · *The Gospel*: Matthew 5:1–12

Baptism

Introduction

This service may be used within Morning or Evening Prayer (after the second Lesson) or within Holy Communion (after the Epistle) on the Lord's Day or a Holy Day. It may be used for both infants and adults. It is recommended that each infant boy should have two male and one female Godparents and each infant girl two female and one male Godparents. Parents may act as Godparents if so desired. Also it is recommended that each adult candidate should have at least one sponsor.

The Minister will normally be a priest but a deacon may also take this service when necessary.

The traditional order of initiation into full and active membership of the Church for infants is (1) Baptism; (2) Being instructed (catechized); (3) Possessing the fruit of faith and repentance; (4) Confirmation and First Communion. In some cases First Communion may precede Confirmation.

The Minister addresses the congregation:

BROTHERS and Sisters in Christ, the Sacrament of Baptism is offered in the Church because our Lord Jesus Christ taught us that we cannot enter the kingdom of God unless we are born anew of water and the Holy Spirit. This new birth is necessary because all human beings have both an inclination towards evil and are also sinners. Therefore, I urge you to call upon God the Father, in the name of our Lord Jesus Christ, that in his great mercy he will grant new birth to this *Child/Person* that he may be baptized with water and the Holy

Baptism

Spirit, and received into Christ's holy Church and be made a living member of the same.

Let us pray.

ALMIGHTY and everlasting God, you who mercifully saved Noah and his family in the Ark when the great flood came, who safely led the children of Israel through the Red Sea, symbolizing thereby your holy Baptism, and who, by the Baptism in the river Jordan of your dearly loved Son, Jesus Christ, sanctified water to the mystical washing away of sin: We pray you, in your infinite mercy, to look on this *Child/Person*, wash and sanctify him by the Holy Spirit, in order that, being delivered from your wrath, he may be received into the Ark of Christ's Church. Make him, we pray, to be steadfast in faith, joyful through hope, and rooted in love, so that passing through the stormy waters of this troubled world, he may finally come to the land of everlasting life, there to reign with you forever; through Jesus Christ our Lord. *Amen.*

ALMIGHTY and immortal God, giver of aid to the needy, strength to the helpless, and everlasting life to those who believe, we pray for this *Child/Person* who is coming to your holy Baptism, that he may receive forgiveness of his sins by spiritual regeneration. Receive him, as you have promised by your dearly loved Son in the Gospel, and make him to come to the eternal kingdom, which you have promised by him who is the Resurrection and the Life, even Jesus Christ our Lord. *Amen.*

Baptism

The congregation stands for the Gospel, which when only infants are being baptized is Mark 10:13–16, and John 3:1–8 when only adults are candidates. And when both Infants and adults are candidates, it is Matthew 28:18–20.

When only Infants are candidates, the following Address may be read.

Brothers and Sisters in Christ, you hear in the Gospel of Mark the words of our Savior Christ commanding the children to be brought to him. You see how he took them in his arms, and blessed them. Jesus Christ is the same yesterday, and today and forever. Do not doubt, therefore, but earnestly believe, that he loves these children, that he approves our bringing of them to holy Baptism, that he is ready to receive them with the arms of his mercy, and to give them the blessing of eternal life.

When only adults are candidates, the following Address may be read.

Brothers and Sisters in Christ, you hear in the Gospel of John the specific words of our Savior Christ that except each one of us is born of water and of the Spirit, we cannot enter into the kingdom of God. You see, therefore, the necessity of this Sacrament. Further, it is recorded at the end of the Gospel of St Mark that: "Whoever believes and is baptized will be saved, but whoever does not believe will be condemned." Jesus Christ is the same yesterday, and today and forever. Do not doubt, therefore, but earnestly believe, that he will favorably receive all who repent of sin and believe the

Baptism

promises of the Gospel; that he will grant them remission of their sins, and bestow on them the Holy Spirit; that he will give them the blessing of eternal life, and that he will make them partakers of his everlasting kingdom.

When both infants and adults are candidates then the Minister may deliver an appropriate Address or Sermon.

After the Address or a Sermon, the Minister says,

BROTHERS and Sisters in Christ, since we are now persuaded of the good will of our heavenly Father towards this *Child/Person*, declared by his Son Jesus Christ, let us faithfully and devoutly give thanks to him, and say together,

ALMIGHTY and everlasting God, heavenly Father, we humbly thank you for having called us to the knowledge of your grace and to faith in you. Increase this knowledge and confirm this faith in us evermore. Give your Holy Spirit to this *Child/Person*, that *he* may be born again, and be made an heir of everlasting salvation; through our Lord Jesus Christ, who lives and reigns with you and the Holy Spirit, now and forever. Amen.

Here a suitable psalm, hymn or spiritual song may be sung.

The parents and godparents stand and the Minister says,

BROTHERS and Sisters in Christ, you have brought this child here to be baptized, you have prayed that our Lord Jesus Christ would be pleased to receive, to cleanse, to sanctify, and to make *him* an heir of the

Baptism

kingdom of heaven and everlasting life. You have heard that our Lord Jesus Christ has promised in the Gospel all these things and we know that he will surely keep his promises.

The adult candidate for Baptism and sponsor stand and the Minister says,

You have come here desirous to be baptized and you have heard how the congregation has prayed that our Lord Jesus Christ would be pleased to receive you and bless you, to forgive your sins and to give you the kingdom of heaven and everlasting life. You have heard also that our Lord Jesus Christ has promised in his holy Word to grant all these things that we have prayed for, and we know that he will surely keep his promises.

The Minister asks the Godparents the following question:

Do you, in the name of this child renounce the devil and all his works, the vain show and glory of this evil world, with all its covetousness, and the sinful desires of human nature, so that you will not follow nor be led by them?
Answer. I renounce them all.

The Minister then asks the adult candidate the following question:

Do you personally renounce the devil and all his works, the vain show and glory of this evil world, with all its covetousness, and the sinful desires of human nature, so that you will not follow nor be led by them?
Answer. I renounce them all.

Baptism

Godparents and adult candidate say with the Minister and congregation the Apostles' Creed.

I BELIEVE in God the Father Almighty, creator of heaven and earth. And I believe in Jesus Christ, his only Son, our Lord. He was conceived by the Holy Spirit and born of the Virgin Mary. He suffered under Pontius Pilate, was crucified, died and was buried. He descended to the dead. On the third day he rose again. He ascended into heaven and sits at the right hand of God the Father Almighty. From there he shall come to judge the living and the dead. I believe in the Holy Spirit, the holy Catholic Church, the communion of saints, the forgiveness of sins, the resurrection of the body and the life everlasting. Amen.

Minister. Do you desire to be baptized in this Faith?
Answer. That is my desire.
Minister. Will you keep God's holy will and commandments, and walk in them all the days of your life?
Answer. I will by God's help.

Then the Minister prays,

MERCIFUL God, grant that this *Child/your Servant* may die to sin, be buried and rise again to eternal life in and with Jesus Christ. *Amen.*

Grant that all sinful desires may die in this *Child/your Servant*, and that all things belonging to the Spirit may live and grow in *him*. *Amen.*

Grant that *he* may have power and strength by faith to have victory, and to triumph against the devil, the world and sinful human nature. *Amen.*

Baptism

Grant that whoever here begins to be a member of your flock may continue in the same forever. *Amen.*

Grant that whoever here is dedicated to you by our office and ministry may also be endued with heavenly virtues, and everlastingly rewarded, through your mercy,

Blessed Lord, who live and govern all things, forever and ever. *Amen.*

At the Font

The Minister standing at the font with the candidates and the Godparents addresses the congregation.

The Lord be with you
People. And with your spirit.
Minister. Lift up your hearts.
People. We lift them to the Lord.
Minister. Let us give thanks to the Lord our God.
People. It is right to give him thanks and praise.

FATHER, almighty and everlasting God, at all times, and in all places, it is good and right to give you thanks and praise: and here we praise you because your most dearly loved Son, for the forgiveness of our sins, shed from his most precious side at the Cross both water and blood; and later gave commandment to his disciples, that they should go teach all nations and baptize them in the Name of the Father, and of the Son and of the Holy Spirit. Hear the prayer of your people;

Baptism

sanctify this water to the mystical washing away of sin; and grant, that this *Child/Person* now to be baptized in it, may receive the fullness of your grace, and ever remain in the number of your faithful and elect children; through Jesus Christ our Lord, to whom with you in the unity of the Holy Spirit, be all honor and glory, now and forever. *Amen.*

The Minister pours water over each candidate and says,

N. I baptize you in the Name of the Father, and of the Son, and of the Holy Spirit. *Amen.*

We receive this *Child/Person* into the congregation of Christ's flock, and sign *him* with the sign of the Cross, in token that from this time forwards *he* shall not be ashamed to confess the faith of Christ crucified, and courageously to fight under his banner against sin, the world and the devil; and to continue Christ's faithful soldier and servant until *his* life's end. *Amen.*

When all have been baptized, the Minister says,

Brothers and Sisters in Christ, now that this *Child/Person* has received the Sacrament of new birth and been received into the family of Christ's Church, let us give thanks unto Almighty God for these benefits; and with one accord make our prayers unto him, that this *Child/Person* may lead the rest of his Christian life according to this good beginning. Let us, as God's children, say together,

Baptism

Traditional

OUR Father who art in heaven, Hallowed be thy Name, Thy kingdom come, Thy will be done, on earth as it is in heaven. Give us this day our daily bread; And forgive us our trespasses, as we forgive them that trespass against us; And lead us not into temptation, but deliver us from evil. For thine is the kingdom, the power and the glory, forever and ever. Amen.

Contemporary

OUR Father in heaven, hallowed be your name. Your kingdom come, your will be done, on earth as in heaven. Give us today our daily bread. Forgive us our sins as we forgive those who sin against us. Lead us not into temptation but deliver us from evil. For yours is the kingdom, and the power, and the glory, forever and ever. Amen.

GRANT, Lord, that being buried with Christ by baptism into his death, this *Child/Person* may also be made partaker of his resurrection; so that, serving you on earth in newness of life, *he* may finally, with the rest of your holy Church, be an inheritor of your everlasting kingdom; through Jesus Christ our Lord. *Amen.*

When a child has been baptized the following prayer may be added here.

Baptism

ALMIGHTY God, our heavenly Father, whose blessed Son shared at Nazareth the life of an earthly home; bless, we pray, the home of this Child, and grant wisdom and understanding to all who have the care of *him*: that *he* may grow up in constant reverence and love of you; through the same Jesus Christ our Lord. *Amen.*

> It is important that either here, or later, the Minister address (a) the Parents and Godparents concerning their responsibilities and duties with respect to the nurture and instruction of the child, including the bringing of the child eventually to Confirmation by the Bishop; and (b) the newly baptized adult concerning Confirmation and First Communion
>
> Here the Service of Morning or Evening Prayer, or of Holy Communion, resumes—unless the short form of Confirmation is to follow—before which the Minister may say the Grace.

The Catechism:
To be learned by every person baptized as a child, before being presented for Confirmation

The young person who is a candidate for Confirmation should be tested in this instruction by the Minister or by a Catechist appointed by the Minister. It is advisable that the candidate learn the answers by heart and have a basic understanding of them, with a clear commitment to their moral and doctrinal content.

Question. What is your Christian Name?

Answer. My Name is *N.N.*

Question. Who gave you this Name?

Answer. My Godfathers and Godmothers in my Baptism, wherein by God's grace I received the sacrament of new birth, entered the family of Christ's Church, and became an inheritor of the kingdom of heaven.

Question. What did your Godfathers and Godmothers do for you at your Baptism?

Answer. They promised and made vows concerning three things in my name. First, that I should renounce the devil and all his works, the pomp and vanity of this wicked world, and all sinful lusts. Secondly, that I should believe all the articles of the Christian Creed. And, thirdly, that I should keep God's holy will and Commandments, walking in them all the days of my life.

Question. Do you think that you are now committed to believe and to do, as they have promised for you?

Answer. Yes, I truly do, and, by God's help, I will. And from the bottom of my heart I thank our heavenly

The Catechism

Father, that he has called me into this enjoyment of salvation, through Jesus Christ our Savior. And I pray to God to give me his grace, that I may continue in this faith to the end of my life.

The Creed

Minister/Catechist. Recite the Apostles' Creed, the Articles of Faith.

I BELIEVE in God the Father Almighty, creator of heaven and earth. And I believe in Jesus Christ, his only Son, our Lord. He was conceived by the Holy Spirit and born of the Virgin Mary. He suffered under Pontius Pilate, was crucified, died and was buried. He descended to the dead. On the third day he rose again. He ascended into heaven and sits at the right hand of God the Father Almighty. From there he shall come to judge the living and the dead. I believe in the Holy Spirit, the holy Catholic Church, the communion of saints, the forgiveness of sins, the resurrection of the body and the life everlasting. Amen.

Question. What important teaching do you learn from these Articles of your Faith?

Answer. First of all, I learn to believe in God the Father, who has made both me and all the world. Secondly, to believe in God the Son, who has redeemed both me and the whole human race. And thirdly, to believe in God the Holy Spirit, who sanctifies both me and all other Christian people.

The Catechism

The Commandments

Question. You stated earlier that your Godfathers and Godmothers promised on your behalf that you would keep God's Commandments. Tell me, how many are there?

Answer. There are ten and they are recorded in the twentieth chapter of the book, Exodus.

Question. What are these Ten Commandments and how are they presented in Exodus?

Answer. We read: God spoke these words and said: I am the LORD your God who brought you out of the land of Egypt, out of the house of slavery;

(1) You shall have no other gods but me.

(2) You shall not make for yourself a carved image, or any likeness of anything that is in heaven above, or that is in the earth below, or that is in the water under the earth.

You shall not bow down to them or serve them, for I the LORD your God am a jealous God, visiting the iniquity of the fathers on the children to the third and fourth generation of those who hate me, but showing steadfast love to thousands of those who love me and keep my commandments.

(3) You shall not take the name of the LORD your God in vain, for the LORD will not hold him guiltless who takes his name in vain.

(4) Remember the Sabbath day, to keep it holy. Six days you shall labor and do all your work, but the seventh day is a Sabbath to the LORD your God. On it you

The Catechism

shall not do any work, you, or your son, or your daughter, your male servant, or your female servant, or your livestock, or the sojourner who is within your gates. For in six days the LORD made heaven and earth, the sea, and all that is in them, and rested the seventh day. Therefore the LORD blessed the Sabbath day and made it holy.

(5) Honor your father and your mother, that your days may be long in the land that the LORD your God is giving you.

(6) You shall not murder.

(7) You shall not commit adultery.

(8) You shall not steal.

(9) You shall not bear false witness against your neighbor.

(10) You shall not covet your neighbor's house, you shall not covet your neighbor's wife, or his male servant, or his female servant, or his ox, or his donkey, or anything that is your neighbor's.

Question. What important teaching do you learn from these Commandments?

Answer. I learn two basic things: my duty towards God, and my duty towards my neighbor.

Question. What is your duty towards God?

Answer: My duty towards God is to believe in him, to be reverent towards him, and to love him, with all my heart, with all my mind, with all my soul, and with all my strength; to worship him, to give him thanks, to put my whole trust in him, to call upon him in

The Catechism

prayer, to honor his holy Name and his Word, and to serve him truly all the days of my life.

Question. What is your duty towards your neighbor?
Answer. My duty towards my neighbor is to love him or her as I love myself, and to do to others as I would have them do unto me. To love, honor and provide for my father and mother: to honor the civil authorities and obey the laws of the State: to submit myself in the Lord to all who have authority over me in home, church, state and education: to conduct myself humbly and appropriately in all my dealings with others, especially with those older than I am: to hurt nobody by either word or deed: to be true and just in all my dealings with others; to bear no malice or hatred in my heart; to keep my hands from pilfering and stealing, and my tongue from speaking evil, telling lies and slandering others; to keep my body under self-restraint, by acting soberly and in purity: not to covet or desire what belongs rightfully to others, and to do my duty where God shall place me today and in the future, and in whatever he calls me to do.

The Lord's Prayer

Minister/Catechist

You need to know that you are not able to do these things in your own strength, and you cannot walk in the Commandments of God and serve him, without his special, gracious help. Therefore, you must learn to ask

The Catechism

for this help from God daily in prayer and especially through the regular saying of the Lord's Prayer.

Question. Can you recite the Lord's Prayer?

Answer. The Lord's Prayer is:

Traditional

Our Father who art in heaven, Hallowed be thy Name, Thy kingdom come, Thy will be done, on earth as it is in heaven. Give us this day our daily bread; And forgive us our trespasses, as we forgive them that trespass against us; And lead us not into temptation, but deliver us from evil. For thine is the kingdom, the power and the glory, forever and ever. Amen.

Contemporary

Our Father in heaven, hallowed be your name. Your kingdom come, your will be done, on earth as in heaven. Give us today our daily bread. Forgive us our sins as we forgive those who sin against us. Lead us not into temptation but deliver us from evil. For yours is the kingdom, and the power, and the glory, forever and ever. Amen.

Question. What do you desire from God in this Prayer?

Answer. I desire my Lord God, our heavenly Father, who is the giver of all goodness, to send his grace to me, and to all people, that we may worship him, serve him, and obey him, as we ought to do. Also I pray to God, that he will send us all that we need both for our souls and bodies; and that he will be merciful to us, and forgive us our sins; and that it will please him to save and defend us in all spiritual and physical dangers; and that he will keep us from all sin and wickedness, from the snares of the devil and from everlasting death. And all this I trust he will do because of his mercy and goodness, through our Lord Jesus Christ. Therefore I say, "Amen, So be it, Lord."

The Sacraments

Question. How many Sacraments has Christ authorized in his Church?

Answer. Two only, Baptism and the Lord's Supper, and these are generally necessary to salvation.

Question. What do you mean when you speak of a Sacrament?

Answer. I mean an outward and visible sign, authorized by Christ, of an inward and spiritual grace given unto us, a way and means whereby we both receive the spiritual grace, and are also given a pledge to assure us of this receiving.

Question. How many parts are there to a Sacrament?

Answer. Two: the outward and visible sign, and the inward and spiritual grace.

Question. What is the outward and visible sign in Baptism?

Answer. Water, in which the person is baptized, "In the Name of the Father, and of the Son, and of the Holy Spirit."

Question. What is the inward and spiritual grace?

The Catechism

Answer. It is being born again of the Holy Spirit and made a child of God by adoption and grace; that is, it is a dying to sin and a new birth into righteousness.

Question. What is required of persons to be baptized?

Answer. Two things: Repentance which is a turning away from sin; and Faith, which is steadfastly believing the promise of God concerning Jesus Christ, proclaimed in the Gospel and the Sacraments.

Question. Why are infants baptized when it is clear that they cannot consciously engage in Repentance and Faith?

Answer. They are baptized on the basis of the promises made on their behalf by their Godparents and in anticipation of their sure acceptance of these same promises when they reach maturity.

Question. Why was the Sacrament of the Lord's Supper ordained by Christ?

Answer. For the continual remembering of the sacrifice of the death of Christ, and of the benefits we receive from this sacrifice.

Question. What is the outward and visible part of the Lord's Supper?

Answer. Bread and wine, which the Lord commanded to be received.

Question. What is the inward and spiritual part, that which is signified by the outward?

Answer. The Body and Blood of Christ, which are really and truly taken and received by the faithful in the Lord's Supper.

The Catechism

Question. What are the benefits received by the faithful by partaking?

Answer. The strengthening and refreshing of our souls by the Body and Blood of Christ, even as our bodies are strengthened and refreshed by the bread and wine.

Question. What is required of those who come to the Lord's Supper?

Answer. They are to examine themselves to be sure that they repent of their sins, are steadfastly intending to lead a new life, have a living faith in God's mercy through Christ, thankfully remember his death, and are loving and charitable to everyone.

The Church and Ministry

Question. When were you made a member of the Church?

Answer. I was made a member of the Church when I was baptized.

Question. What is the Church?

Answer. The Church is the Body of which Jesus Christ is the Head, and all baptized people are the members.

Question. How is the Church described in the Apostles' and Nicene Creeds?

Answer. The Church is described in the Creeds as One, Holy, Catholic and Apostolic.

Question. What do we mean by these words?

Answer. We mean that the Church is One, because it is one Body under one Head: Holy, because the Holy

The Catechism

Spirit dwells within it and sanctifies its members: Catholic, because it is universal, holding sincerely the Faith for all time, in all countries, and for all people; and is sent to preach the Gospel to the whole world: Apostolic, because it continues firmly in the Apostles' teaching and fellowship.

Question. What is your binding duty as a member of the Church?

Answer. My binding duty is to follow Christ, to worship God every Sunday in his Church, and to work and pray and give for the spread of his kingdom.

Question. What special means does the Church provide to help you to do all these things?

Answer. The Church provides the Laying on of hands, or Confirmation. Here, after renewing the promises and vows of my Baptism, and declaring my loyalty and devotion to Christ as my Master, I receive the gifts of the Holy Spirit to give me inner strength.

Question. After you have been confirmed, what great privilege does our Lord provide for you?

Answer. Our Lord provides the Sacrament of the Lord's Supper, or Holy Communion, for the continual strengthening and refreshing of my soul.

Question. What orders of Ministers are there in the Church?

Answer. Bishops, Priests, and Deacons; which orders have been in the Church from the earliest times.

Question. What is the office of a Bishop?

Answer. The office of a Bishop is to be a chief Pastor in

The Catechism

the Church; to confer Holy Orders; and to administer Confirmation.

Question. What is the office of a Priest?

Answer. The office of a Priest is to minister to the people committed to his care; to preach the Word of God; to baptize; to celebrate the Holy Communion; and to pronounce Absolution and Blessing in God's Name.

Question. What is the office of a Deacon?

Answer. The office of a Deacon is to assist the Priest in Divine Service, and in his other ministrations, under the direction of the Bishop.

Minister/Catechist.

Let us conclude in prayer

GRANT to us, heavenly Father, we humbly ask of you, the spirit to think and to do always such things as are right in your sight. Without your help, we cannot do anything that is truly good, and so we sincerely pray that in your strength we shall be able to live according to your will; through Jesus Christ our Lord. *Amen.*

Confirmation

A shortened form to accompany the Baptism of Adults

The Minister addresses the Bishop:

Reverend Father in God, I present to you these persons to receive the laying on of hands.

Then the Bishop says:

Our help is in the name of the Lord.
Answer. Who has made heaven and earth.
The Bishop. Blessed be the Name of the Lord.
Answer. Always and *forever*.
The Bishop. Lord, hear our prayer;
Answer. And let our cry come unto you.
The Bishop. Let us pray.

ALMIGHTY and ever-living God, by whose grace these your servants have been born again of water and the Spirit, and have received forgiveness of all their sins; confirm and strengthen them with the Holy Spirit, the Comforter, and daily increase in them your plentiful gifts of grace; the spirit of wisdom and understanding; the spirit of guidance and strength; the spirit of knowledge and true godliness; and fill them, Lord, with the spirit of your holy fear, both now and forever. *Amen.*

Those to be confirmed kneel before the Bishop who lays his hands upon the head of each and prays one of the following prayers:

Confirmation

CONFIRM and defend, Lord, this your servant N. with your heavenly grace, that *he* may continue yours forever; and daily increase in your Holy Spirit, more and more, until *he* comes to your everlasting kingdom. *Amen.*

or

STRENGTHEN, Lord, your servant *N.* with your Holy Spirit; empower *him* for your service; and sustain *him* all the days of *his* life. *Amen.*

When there are those present who come from other Christian bodies to be received into membership, then each kneels before the Bishop who says:

N. we recognize you as a member of the one, holy, catholic and apostolic Church, and we receive you into the membership of this Communion. May God the Father, the Son and the Holy Spirit, bless, preserve and keep you. *Amen.*

Confirmation or Laying on of Hands on those who are baptized and are ready to declare publicly their commitment to Christ

All those to be confirmed stand before the Bishop, and either he or another Minister reads these introductory words:

THE Church requires that all who come to Confirmation should know the Apostles' Creed, the Lord's Prayer and the Ten Commandments, and have a basic understanding of the Christian Faith as received in the Church.

We intend to administer the laying on of hands to

Confirmation

these persons who by baptism are members of Christ's Church and are prepared for Confirmation through instruction and prayer. We do so for three reasons:

First, because it is evident from the Holy Scripture that the Apostles laid their hands upon those who were baptized; and this practice has been continued in the Church since the Apostles' time and has been judged agreeable to Holy Scripture.

Secondly, so that persons, having come to the years of discretion, may acknowledge publicly the vows made at their Baptism, and dedicate their lives to serving our Lord Jesus Christ.

Thirdly, in order that by prayer and the laying on of hands, they may be strengthened by the Holy Spirit, courageously to fight under the banner of Christ crucified, against sin, the world and the devil, and to continue Christ's faithful soldiers and servants to the end of their lives.

Then the Bishop asks those who have come to Confirmation:

Do you here, in the presence of God and this congregation, renew the solemn promise and vow made in your name or by you at your Baptism?
Answer. I do.

Then the Bishop says:

Our help is in the name of the Lord.
Answer. Who has made heaven and earth.
The Bishop. Blessed be the Name of the Lord.

Confirmation

Answer. Always and forever.
The Bishop. Lord, hear our prayer.
Answer. And let our cry come unto you.

The Bishop continues in prayer:

ALMIGHTY and ever-living God, by whose grace these your servants have been born again of water and the Spirit, and have received forgiveness of all their sins; confirm and strengthen them with the Holy Spirit, the Comforter, and daily increase in them your plentiful gifts of grace; the spirit of wisdom and understanding; the spirit of guidance and strength; the spirit of knowledge and true godliness; and fill them, Lord, with the spirit of your holy fear, both now and forever. *Amen.*

Those to be confirmed kneel before the Bishop who lays his hands upon the head of each and prays one of the following prayers:

CONFIRM and defend, Lord, this your servant N. with your heavenly grace, that *he* may continue yours forever; and daily increase in your Holy Spirit, more and more, until *he* comes to your everlasting kingdom. *Amen.*

or

STRENGTHEN, Lord, your servant N. with your Holy Spirit; empower *him* for your service; and sustain *him* all the days of his/her life. *Amen.*

Confirmation

When there are those present who come from other Christian bodies to be received into membership, then each kneels before the Bishop who says:

N. we recognize you as a member of the one, holy, catholic and apostolic Church, and we receive you into the membership of this Communion. May God the Father, the Son and the Holy Spirit, bless, preserve and keep you. *Amen*

Then the Bishop says,

The Lord be with you.
Answer. And with your spirit.
The Bishop. Let us pray,

Traditional

Our Father who art in heaven, Hallowed be thy Name, Thy kingdom come, Thy will be done, on earth as it is in heaven. Give us this day our daily bread; And forgive us our trespasses, as we forgive them that trespass against us; And lead us not into temptation, but deliver us from evil. For thine is the kingdom, the power and the glory, forever and ever. Amen.

Contemporary

Our Father in heaven, hallowed be your name. Your kingdom come, your will be done, on earth as in heaven. Give us today our daily bread. Forgive us our sins as we forgive those who sin against us. Lead us not into temptation but deliver us from evil. For yours is the kingdom, and the power, and the glory, forever and ever. Amen.

Confirmation

The Bishop prays,

ALMIGHTY and ever-living God, you who make us both to will and to do those things that are good and acceptable in your sight; we humbly pray for these your servants upon whom, after the example of your holy apostles, hands have been laid, to assure them, by this sign, of your favor and gracious goodness towards them. Let your fatherly hand, we pray, always be over them; let your Holy Spirit always be with them; and so lead them in the knowledge and obedience of your Word, that in the end they may obtain everlasting life; through our Lord Jesus Christ, who with you and the Holy Spirit lives and reigns, one God, now and forever. *Amen.*

ALMIGHTY and everlasting God, be pleased, we pray, to direct, sanctify, and govern our souls and bodies in the ways of your laws and in the obeying of your commandments; and grant that, through your most mighty protection, we may be preserved, in body and soul, now and always, through our Lord and Savior Jesus Christ. *Amen.*

Then the Bishop blesses the newly-confirmed.

GO forth into the world in peace; be of good courage; hold fast to that which is good; render to no person evil for evil; strengthen the fainthearted; support the weak; help the afflicted; honor all people; love and serve the Lord, rejoicing in the power of the Holy Spirit. And the Blessing of God Almighty, the Father, the Son and the Holy Spirit, be upon you, and remain with you always. *Amen.*

The Solemnization of Holy Matrimony

(The Celebration and Blessing of a Marriage)

The Service may begin with the bridal procession accompanied by suitable music, after which a psalm, hymn or spiritual song may be sung.

The congregation sits and the Minister reads the following Introduction, as the man and woman stand before him, the man on his left and the woman on his right.

WE have gathered here in the sight of God and in the presence of this congregation to join together this man and this woman in marriage.

Marriage is an honorable, ordered relation and state instituted by God in the time before man and woman sinned. It signifies the mystical union between Christ and his Church. Christ adorned and beautified this ordered relation with both his presence and first miracle that he performed at a marriage in Cana of Galilee. Further, it is commended in Holy Scripture to be respected by all, and, therefore, it must not be entered upon, nor taken in hand, unadvisedly or lightly, but reverently, discreetly, advisedly, soberly, and in the fear of God; duly considering the causes for which marriage was ordained by God.

First, it was ordained for the procreation of children, to be brought up in the fear and nurture of the Lord, and to the praise of his holy Name.

Secondly, it was ordained that the natural instincts

Marriage

and affections, implanted by God in man and woman, should be hallowed and directed aright.

Thirdly, it was ordained for the mutual companionship, help, and comfort that husband and wife should provide for one another both in prosperity and adversity.

These two persons have come to be joined together in this holy relation and state. Therefore, if anyone can show any just cause why they may not be lawfully joined together, let that person now speak.

If no impediment is alleged, the Minister says to the man and woman:

I CHARGE you both, as you will answer before God on the day of judgment when the secrets of all our hearts will be disclosed, that if either of you knows of any reason why you may not lawfully be joined together in marriage, you must now declare it. Further, each of you must recognize that those who marry contrary to what God's Word allows are not joined together by God, and neither is their marriage lawful before him.

If no impediment is stated, the Minister says to the man,

N. will you take this woman *N.* as your wife, to live together as God has ordained. Will you live daily in sacrificial love for her, comfort her, honor and protect her, in sickness and in health; and forsaking all others, be faithful to her as long as you both shall live?

Marriage

The man answers,

I will.

N. Will you take N. as your husband and live together as God has ordained? Will you love him, submit to him, honor him, and protect him, in sickness and in health; and, forsaking all others, be faithful to him as long as you both shall live?

The woman answers,

I will.

Then the Minister may say,

Who gives this woman to be married to this man?

The Minister receives the bride's right hand from her father, or from another person, and passes it to the bridegroom, who takes her right hand in his right hand.

All stand to witness the marriage vows.

The bridegroom, holding the bride's right hand in his right hand, says:

I N. take you N. to be my wife, to have and to hold from this day forward, for better for worse, for richer for poorer, in sickness and in health, to love and to cherish, until we are parted by death, according to God's holy law; and this is my solemn vow.

They loose hands and the bride takes the bridegroom's right hand in her right hand and says:

Marriage

I *N.* take you *N.* to be my husband, to have and to hold from this day forward, for better for worse, for richer for poorer, in sickness and in health, to love, cherish, and obey, until we are parted by death, according to God's holy law; and this is my solemn vow.

> They loose hands, and the bridegroom places the wedding ring on the Minister's book and he may then bless the ring. The bridegroom then takes the ring and places it on the fourth finger of the left hand of the bride. He holds the ring in place and then repeats the following words after the Minister.

I GIVE you this ring as a sign of our marriage. With my body I honor you, all that I am I give to you, and all that I have I share with you: in the name of the Father and of the Son and of the Holy Spirit. Amen.

> (If there is a second ring given by the bride to the bridegroom, the Minister may bless it before she takes it and says:
> **This ring I give you in token and pledge of my constant faith and abiding love.**)

> The couple kneel as the Minister prays for them:

E TERNAL God, our Creator and Preserver, Giver of all spiritual grace, and Author of everlasting life, send your blessing upon your servants, *N.* and *N.*, whom we bless in your Name. Grant that, as Isaac and Rebecca lived faithfully together, so they may surely fulfill and keep the vow and covenant they have made, of which this ring is (*or* these rings are) a token and pledge. May they ever remain in perfect love and peace together as

Marriage

they live according to your holy laws; through Jesus Christ our Lord. *Amen.*

Then the Minister places their right hands together and says,

Those whom God has joined together let no one put asunder.

The Minister addresses all the people.

N. and *N.* have consented together in holy matrimony and have witnessed the same before God and this congregation. They have made their vows to one another and have declared their marriage by the giving and exchanging of a ring/rings and the joining of hands. I therefore pronounce that they are husband and wife together; in the Name of the Father, and of the Son, and of the Holy Spirit. *Amen.*

The Minister now blesses the husband and wife.

God the Father, God the Son, God the Holy Spirit, bless, preserve, and keep you; the Lord mercifully with his favor look upon you, and so fill you with all spiritual benediction and grace, that you may so live together in this life, that in the world to come you may have everlasting life. *Amen.*

A Lesson from the Holy Scriptures may be read, followed by an Address, as the congregation sits.

The husband and wife kneel before the Holy Table and the Minister leads the congregation in prayer.

Marriage

Lord have mercy upon us.
Christ have mercy upon us.
Lord have mercy upon us.

Then all may say the Lord's Prayer.

Traditional

OUR Father who art in heaven, Hallowed be thy Name, Thy kingdom come, Thy will be done, on earth as it is in heaven. Give us this day our daily bread; And forgive us our trespasses, as we forgive them that trespass against us; And lead us not into temptation, but deliver us from evil. For thine is the kingdom, the power and the glory, forever and ever. Amen.

Contemporary

OUR Father in heaven, hallowed be your name. Your kingdom come, your will be done, on earth as in heaven. Give us today our daily bread. Forgive us our sins as we forgive those who sin against us. Lead us not into temptation but deliver us from evil. For yours is the kingdom, and the power, and the glory, forever and ever. Amen.

Minister: Lord, save this man and his wife;
People: Who put their trust in you.
Minister: Lord, send them help from heaven;
People: And defend them now and always.
Minister: Be to them a tower of strength,
People: In the face of all evil and danger.
Minister: Lord, hear our prayer;
People: And let our cry come unto you.

Marriage

The Minister continues,

GOD of Abraham, Isaac, and Jacob, bless *N.* and *N.* by sowing the seed of eternal life in their hearts; so that whatever they profitably learn from your holy Word they may indeed fulfill. Look mercifully upon them from heaven, Lord God, and bless them as you blessed Abraham and Sarah in ancient times, so that, obeying your will, and safe and secure in your protection, they may remain in your love to the end of their lives; through Jesus Christ our Lord. *Amen.*

One or more of the following prayers may be used:

MERCIFUL Lord and heavenly Father, by whose gracious gift the human race is increased, bestow, we humbly pray, upon these two persons the heritage and gift of children; and grant that they may live together so long in godly life and honesty, that they may see their children brought up in Christian faith and virtue, to your praise and honor; through Jesus Christ our Lord. *Amen.*

ALMIGHTY God, you who by your mighty power created all things both out of nothing and in an orderly way; who then created the man, and woman out of man, and both in your image and likeness; and who also taught that marriage is a life-long union, which never should be broken; hear our prayer for these your servants that they may take to heart these truths and be strengthened by them.

Holy God, you who have so elevated the state of marriage that in it is symbolized and represented the

Marriage

spiritual union between Christ, the Bridegroom, and his Church, the Bride: Look in mercy, we pray, upon these your servants, that this man. *N.* may love his wife according to your Word (imitating the way in which Christ loved and cherished the Church and gave himself for her); and also that this woman, *N.* may be loving and pleasant, faithful and obedient to her husband; and in all quietness, sobriety, and peace, imitate holy and godly wives and mothers who have gone before her. Be pleased to bless them both, and grant that they will inherit your everlasting kingdom; through Jesus Christ our Lord. *Amen.*

MAY Almighty God, who created our first parents, Adam and Eve, at the beginning of the world, and then caused them to be joined together in marriage, pour upon you the riches of his grace, sanctify and bless you, that you may please him both in body and soul to the end of your lives. *Amen.*

> If there has not been an address declaring the duties of husband and wife, the following may be read.

HEAR what the Holy Scripture says about the duty of husbands towards their wives, first from Saint Paul and then from Saint Peter, himself a married man.

"Husbands, love your wives, as Christ loved the church and gave himself up for her, that he might sanctify her, having cleansed her by the washing of water with the word, so that he might present the church to himself in splendor, without spot or wrinkle or any such thing, that she might be holy and without blemish.

Marriage

In the same way husbands should love their wives as their own bodies. He who loves his wife loves himself. For no one ever hated his own flesh, but nourishes and cherishes it, just as Christ does the church, because we are members of his body. Therefore a man shall leave his father and mother and hold fast to his wife, and the two shall become one flesh. This mystery is profound, and I am saying that it refers to Christ and the church. However, let each one of your love his wife as himself" (Ephesians 5:25–33).

And:

"Husbands love your wives and do not be harsh with them" (Colossians 3:19).

"Husbands, live with your wives in an understanding way, showing honor to the women as the weaker vessel, since they are heirs with you of the grace of life, so that your prayers may not be hindered" (1 Peter 3:7).

Hear now what the Holy Scripture says about the duty of wives to their husbands, first from Saint Paul and then from Saint Peter.

"Wives, submit yourselves to your own husbands, as to the Lord. For the husband is the head of the wife even as Christ is the head of the church, his body, and is himself its Savior. Now as the church submits to Christ, so also wives should submit to their husbands" (Ephesians 5:22–24).

And,

"Wives, submit to your husbands, as is fitting in the Lord" (Colossians 3:18).

Marriage

And,

"Wives, be subject to your own husbands, so that even if some do not obey the word, they may be won without a word by the conduct of their wives—when they see your respectful and pure conduct. Do not let your adorning be external—the braiding of hair, the wearing of gold, or the putting on of clothing—but let your adorning be the hidden person of the heart with the imperishable beauty of a gentle and quiet spirit, which in God's sight is very precious. For this is how the holy women, who hoped in God, used to adorn themselves, by submitting to their husbands, as Sarah obeyed Abraham, calling him lord. And you are her children, if you do good and do not fear anything that is frightening" (1 Peter 3:1–6).

If the Service of Holy Communion is to follow immediately, then a psalm, hymn or spiritual song may be sung. If it does not follow, then the newly married couple are urged to receive Holy Communion together at the first convenient occasion.

If there is to be Holy Communion the following Collect, Epistle and Gospel are used at it:

GOD our Father, who by your holy apostle Paul have taught us that love is the fulfilling of the law: Grant to these your servants that, loving one another, they may continue in your love to the end of their lives; through Jesus Christ, our Lord, who lives and reigns

Marriage

with you in the unity of the Holy Spirit, one God, world without end. *Amen.*

Epistle: Ephesians 3: 14–19 · *Gospel:* John 15: 9–12

If there is no Service of Holy Communion, the Marriage Service ends here in an appropriate way, e.g., with a procession through and out of the church, led by the newly married couple.

Visitation of the Sick

The whole of this Service, or parts of it, may be used when visiting a sick person at home, in hospital, or other care center.

On entering the sick person's room, the Minister says:

LET the Peace of God be present in this house and with all who live here.

Or

Let the Peace of God be known in this room and with all who are present here.

Let us pray.

Lord, have mercy upon us,
Christ have mercy upon us,
Lord, have mercy upon us.

Traditional

OUR Father who art in heaven, Hallowed be thy Name, Thy kingdom come, Thy will be done, on earth as it is in heaven. Give us this day our daily bread; And forgive us our trespasses, as we forgive them that trespass against us; And lead us not into temptation, but deliver us from evil. For thine is the kingdom, the power and the glory, forever and ever. Amen.

Contemporary

OUR Father in heaven, hallowed be your name. Your kingdom come, your will be done, on earth as in heaven. Give us today our daily bread. Forgive us our sins as we forgive those who sin against us. Lead us not into temptation but deliver us from evil. For yours is the kingdom, and the power, and the glory, forever and ever. Amen.

Visitation of the Sick

Lord our God, we ask you to look down from heaven to see, visit and relieve this your servant, *N*. Look upon *him* with the eyes of your mercy, give *him* comfort and sure confidence in you; defend *him* in all danger, and keep *him* in continual peace and safety; through Jesus Christ, our Lord. *Amen.*

> A suitable passage from the New Testament may be read here: e.g., Matthew 9:2–8; Luke 17:11–19; 2 Corinthians 1:3–5; Hebrews 12:1–2.
>
> Then one or more of the following Psalms, or parts thereof, may be used: 3, 43, 77, 138, and 103. Between the Psalms, or after them, one or both of the following Collects may be used.

Sanctify, we pray you, O Lord our God, the sickness of this your servant to personal holiness, that the sense of *his* weakness may add strength to *his* faith and seriousness to *his* repentance; and grant that *he* may dwell with you in life everlasting; through Jesus Christ our Lord. *Amen.*

God, our Father, the Strength of the weak and the Comfort of those who suffer; mercifully accept our prayers, and grant the help of your Holy Spirit to your servant, that *his* sickness may be turned into health, and our sorrow into joy; through Jesus Christ our Lord. *Amen.*

Savior of the world, you who by your Cross and precious Blood have redeemed us; Save us, and help us, we humbly pray you, O Lord.

Visitation of the Sick

Here, when appropriate, the Minister may speak to the sick person on the meaning and use of sickness, and the opportunity if offers for spiritual profit, when seen within the good providence of God.

Also the Minister may ask the sick person about his acceptance of the Christian Faith, and whether he truly repents of his sins and loves his neighbor as himself. Further, he may urge him to forgive, from the bottom of his heart, all persons who have offended him; and, if he has offended any, to ask of them forgiveness; and where he has done injury or wrong to any person, that he make full amends.

Finally, opportunity for the sick person to make a special confession of his sins should be provided; and where this occurs it should be followed by the assurance of mercy and forgiveness declared by the Minister. The Absolution may take this form:

ALMIGHTY God, our heavenly Father, have mercy upon you, forgive you all your sins, deliver you from all evil, preserve and strengthen you in all goodness, and bring you to everlasting life; through Jesus Christ our Lord. *Amen.*

Then the Minister says:

Let us pray,

MOST merciful God, you who, according to your abundant mercy, put away the sins of those who truly repent so that you remember them no more: Be merciful to this your servant, who most sincerely desires your forgiveness. Renew in *him,* most loving Father, whatever has been distorted by the fraud and malice of the devil, or by *his* own disobedient will and

Visitation of the Sick

frailty; preserve and retain *him* in the unity of the Church; consider *his* contrition, accept *his* tears and relieve *his* pain, according to your perfect will. And, in that *he* puts *his* full trust only in your mercy, do not reckon to *him his* former sins but the righteousness of Christ, and strengthen *him* with your Holy Spirit. Finally, when you are pleased to take *him* from us, take *him* into your heavenly favor; through the merit of your most dearly-loved Son, Jesus Christ our Lord. *Amen.*

THE Almighty Lord, who is the perfect source of strength to all who put their trust in him, and is the One to whom all things in heaven and earth bow and obey; Be now and always your defense; and make you know and feel that the only Name under heaven given to man, in whom, and through whom, you may receive health and salvation, is the precious Name of our Lord Jesus Christ. *Amen.*

> Here may be administered, if desired and appropriate, either the Laying on of hands or the Anointing with oil. It may be prefaced by the reading of James 5:13–15 or Mark 6:7, 12–13 or Psalm 2; and the following prayers and declarations may be used.
>
> For Laying on of hands the following prayer and declaration may be used:

ALMIGHTY Father, whose blessed Son laid his hands upon the sick to heal them: Grant, we pray, to this your servant, on whom we now lay our hands in his Name, refreshment of spirit, and, according to your

Visitation of the Sick

gracious will, restoration to health of body and mind; through Jesus Christ our Lord. *Amen.*

I lay my hands on you in the Name of our Savior Jesus Christ, asking him, that through his merits and precious death, he will grant you forgiveness of your sins, relief from your pains, and recovery of health in mind and body, to the glory of his Name. *Amen.*

For Anointing the following prayer and declaration may be used.

LORD Jesus Christ, Redeemer of the world, relieve, we pray you, by the inward anointing of the Holy Spirit, the distress of this your servant. Release *him* from sin, drive away all pain of mind and body; restore *him* to soundness of health; and grant that *he* may always give to you, together with the Father and the Holy Spirit, praise and thanksgiving in your holy Church forever and ever. *Amen.*

I anoint you with oil in the Name of the Father, and of the Son, and of the Holy Spirit; praying for the mercy of our Lord Jesus Christ, that all your pain and sickness of body being put to flight, the blessing of health may be restored to you. *Amen.*

When there is no Laying on of hands or Anointing with oil, further prayers may be offered and the Visitation ends with this blessing pronounced by the Minister.

UNTO God's gracious mercy and protection we commit you. The Lord bless you, and keep you; The Lord make his face shine upon you, and be gracious to

Visitation of the Sick

you. The Lord turn his face to you and give you peace, both now and always. *Amen.*

> After the Visitation there may follow The Communion of the Sick.

Further Prayers

> Any of these prayers may be used in the Visitation of the Sick according to the discretion of the Minister.

ALMIGHTY God, the giver of all health and the true aid to all who turn to you for support; we earnestly seek your strength and goodness on behalf of this your servant, that *he* may be healed of *his* infirmities, to your honor and glory; through Jesus Christ our Lord. *Amen.*

LORD and heavenly Father, you who relieve those who suffer in soul and body; stretch out your hand, we pray you, to heal your servant N., and to ease *his* pain; that by your mercy *he* may be restored to health of body and mind, and reveal *his* thankfulness both in love to you and service of *his* fellow human beings; through Jesus Christ our Lord. *Amen.*

LORD Jesus Christ, great Physician of your people, look with your gracious favor upon this your servant; give wisdom and skill to those who minister to *him* in *his* sickness; bless all the means used for *his* recovery; stretch out your hand, and, according to your will, restore *him* to health and strength, that *he* may live to praise you for your goodness and your grace; to the glory of your holy Name. *Amen.*

The Burial of the Dead

Introduction

The purpose of this Service is to proclaim the Christian faith and hope in which the body of the person to be buried, or cremated and interred, has died. It is only to be used for the baptized. Comfort is presented to the mourners in their loss of the loved one by the strong promises of the Gospel. As this is not a memorial service, it is not usually appropriate to add to it statements or presentations about the life and achievements of the deceased.

This Service is intended for use in a Burial Ground or in Church and Burial Ground. Where it is used in a Funeral Home or for Cremation, there will need to be some adjustment of the order or content and perhaps some minor modification of the text.

The Minister (with assistants and the choir) meets the body and mourners at the entrance to the church, chapel or burial ground, and says or sings some or all of the following Sentences; also one or more of the Penitential Psalms (6, 32, 38, 51, 102, 130 & 143) or parts thereof may be said or sung.

"I AM the resurrection and the life," says the Lord Jesus. "Whoever believes in me, though he die, yet shall he live, and everyone who lives and believes in me shall never die." *John 11:25*

For I know that my Redeemer lives, and at the last he will stand upon the earth. And after my skin has been destroyed, in my flesh I shall see God, whom I shall see for myself, and my eyes shall behold him, and not another. *Job 19:25*

We brought nothing into the world and we cannot

The Burial of the Dead

take anything out of the world. The Lord gave and the Lord has taken away: blessed be the Name of the Lord. *1 Timothy 6:7 & Job 1:21*

Remember not the sins of my youth or my transgressions; according to your steadfast love remember me, for the sake of your goodness, Lord. *Psalm 25:6*

The eternal God is your dwelling place, and underneath you are the everlasting arms. *Deuteronomy 33:27*

Neither death nor life, nor angels nor rulers, nor things present nor things to come, nor powers, nor height nor depth, nor anything else in all creation, will be able to separate us from the love of God in Christ Jesus our Lord. *Romans 8:38*

If we live, we live to the Lord, and if we die, we die to the Lord. So, then, whether we live or whether we die, we are the Lord's. *Romans 14:8*

Let not your hearts be troubled, believe in God, believe also in me. In my Father's house are many rooms... I go to prepare a place for you. *John 14:1*

When everyone is in place, one or more of these Psalms may be said or sung: 39, 90, 23 & 130.

Then a hymn or spiritual song may be sung.

The Lesson is read from 1 Corinthians 15:20–58 (verses 27–34 may be omitted); as an alternative John 14, 1–6; or 2 Corinthians 4:15 – 5:10; or Revelation 7:9–17; or Revelation 21:1–7 may be read.

Then may follow The Apostles' Creed.

I BELIEVE in God the Father Almighty, creator of heaven and earth. And I believe in Jesus Christ, his only

The Burial of the Dead

Son, our Lord. He was conceived by the Holy Spirit and born of the Virgin Mary. He suffered under Pontius Pilate, was crucified, died and was buried. He descended to the dead. On the third day he rose again. He ascended into heaven and sits at the right hand of God the Father Almighty. From there he shall come to judge the living and the dead. I believe in the Holy Spirit, the holy Catholic Church, the communion of saints, the forgiveness of sins, the resurrection of the body and the life everlasting. Amen.

> Immediately following the Lesson or Creed, a homily may be preached, proclaiming the Christian Hope contained in the Gospel of the Father concerning his Son, the Lord Jesus Christ, and salvation into eternal life through him.
>
> Then a hymn or spiritual song may be sung, and after it suitable prayers may be said.
>
> The Grace, or one of the following Blessings, may be used here to close the first part of the Service.

THE Lord bless you, and keep you. The Lord make his face to shine upon you, and be gracious to you. The Lord turn his face towards you, and give you peace, now and always. *Amen.*

THE God of peace, who through the blood of the eternal covenant brought back from the dead our Lord Jesus, that great Shepherd of the sheep, equip you with everything good for doing his will, working in what is pleasing to him, through Jesus Christ, to whom be glory forever and ever. *Amen.*

The Burial of the Dead

The rest of the service takes place at the graveside; but all or part of it may be held in the church or chapel, as occasion or necessity require.

At the Graveside

The Minister says:

In the midst of life we are in death; Whom may we seek as our helper, but you, O Lord, who for our sins are justly displeased?

Holy God, holy and mighty, holy and merciful Savior, deliver us not into the bitter pains of eternal death.

You know, O Lord, the secrets of our hearts; do not close your merciful ears to our prayer; but spare us, most holy Lord, most mighty God, holy and merciful Savior, most worthy eternal Judge; do not allow us, at our last hour, for any pains of eternal death, to fall from you.

Or this, from Psalm 103:13–17,

As a father shows compassion to his children, so the Lord shows compassion on those who fear him.

For he knows our frame; he remembers that we are dust.

As for man, his days are like grass, he flourishes like a flower of the field;

For the wind passes over it, and it is gone, and its place knows it no more.

But the steadfast love of the Lord is from everlasting to everlasting on those who fear him, and his righteousness to children's children.

The Burial of the Dead

As the body is being lowered into the grave and earth cast upon it, the Minister says,

SINCE it has pleased Almighty God of his great mercy to take unto himself the soul of our dear brother/sister, who has departed this life; we therefore commit his/her body to the ground; earth to earth; ashes to ashes; dust to dust; in sure and certain hope of the Resurrection to eternal life, through our Lord Jesus Christ; who shall change our earthly, weak body, that it may be like his own glorious body, according to the mighty working of his Spirit, whereby he is able to subdue all things to himself. *Amen.*

Then the following is said or sung,

I HEARD a voice from heaven saying, "Write this: Blessed are the dead who die in the Lord from now on." "Blessed indeed," says the Spirit, "that they may rest from their labors, for their deeds shall follow them."

Then shall the Minister say,

The Lord be with you.
Answer: And with your spirit.
Let us pray.
Lord, have mercy upon us.
Christ, have mercy upon us.
Lord, have mercy upon us.

The Burial of the Dead

Traditional

Our Father who art in heaven, Hallowed be thy Name, Thy kingdom come, Thy will be done, on earth as it is in heaven. Give us this day our daily bread; And forgive us our trespasses, as we forgive them that trespass against us; And lead us not into temptation, but deliver us from evil. For thine is the kingdom, the power and the glory, forever and ever. Amen.

Contemporary

Our Father in heaven, hallowed be your name. Your kingdom come, your will be done, on earth as in heaven. Give us today our daily bread. Forgive us our sins as we forgive those who sin against us. Lead us not into temptation but deliver us from evil. For yours is the kingdom, and the power, and the glory, forever and ever. Amen.

Almighty God, we rejoice that the spirits of those who have departed this life in the faith of Christ live with you, and that the souls of the faithful, after they are delivered from the burden of this earthly life, are in joy and blessedness: We give you most sincere thanks, for it has pleased you to deliver this our brother/sister out of the miseries of this sinful world and take him/her to yourself. Also, we ask you, in your great goodness, that it may please you to bring to completion the number of your chosen children and to hasten the coming of your kingdom, so that, together with all who have departed this life in the true faith of your holy Name, we may

The Burial of the Dead

be made perfect in body and soul in your eternal glory, through Jesus Christ our Lord. *Amen.*

MERCIFUL God, the Father of our Lord Jesus Christ, who is the Resurrection and the Life, we rejoice that whoever believes in Christ, though he die, yet shall he live, and that everyone who lives and believes in him shall never die. We also rejoice that you have also taught us (by the holy apostle Saint Paul) not to be sorry, as people without hope, for all those who have died in the faith of Christ and sleep in him. So we humbly ask you, Father, to raise us from the death of sin to the life of righteousness; that, when we depart this life, we may rest in Christ, as our hope is that this our brother/sister does; and that, at the general Resurrection in the last day, we may be found acceptable in your sight, and receive that blessing, which your well-beloved Son shall then pronounce upon all that love and reverence you, as he will say, "Come, blessed children of my Father, receive the kingdom prepared for you from the beginning of the world." Grant all this, merciful Father, through Jesus Christ, our Mediator and Redeemer. *Amen.*

THE grace of our Lord Jesus Christ, and the love of God, and the fellowship of the Holy Spirit, be with us all evermore. *Amen.*

Further directions

> If the ground where the grave is dug is not consecrated, the Minister on coming to the grave may first say this prayer:

The Burial of the Dead

ALMIGHTY God, the Father of our Lord Jesus Christ, be pleased, we pray you, to bless this grave to be the peaceful resting-place of the body of your servant; through the same your blessed Son, who is the resurrection and the life, and who lives and reigns with you and the Holy Spirit, forever and ever. *Amen.*

> When there is a special celebration of Holy Communion on the day of the Burial, the Collect is to be that appointed for Easter Eve; the Epistle to be either 1 Thessalonians 4:13–18 or 2 Corinthians 4:16 to 5:4; and the Gospel to be either John 6:37–41 or John 5:24–29.
>
> The following prayers may be used either at the graveside or earlier.

ALMIGHTY God, Father of all mercies and giver of all comfort; Deal graciously, we pray, with those who mourn, that casting every care upon you, they may know the power of your love to console them; through Jesus Christ our Lord. *Amen.*

HEAVENLY Father, whose Blessed Son Jesus Christ wept at the grave of Lazarus, his friend; Look with compassion upon those who are now in sorrow and affliction; comfort them, Lord, with your consoling love; make them to know that in all things you work for the good of those who love you; and grant them always sure trust and confidence in your fatherly care; through the same Jesus Christ our Lord. *Amen.*

Interment or Scattering of Ashes

The Minister or another person reads the following:

I AM sure that neither death nor life, nor angels nor rulers, nor things present nor things to come, nor powers, nor height nor depth, nor anything else in all creation, will be able to separate us from the love of God in Christ Jesus our Lord. *Romans 8:38–39*

I lift up my eyes to the hills. From where does my help come?

My help comes from the Lord, who made heaven and earth.

He will not let your foot be moved; he who keeps you will not slumber.

Behold, he who keeps Israel will neither slumber nor sleep.

The Lord is your keeper; the Lord is your shade on your right hand.

The sun shall not strike you by day, nor the moon by night.

The Lord will keep you from all evil; he will keep your life.

The Lord will keep your going out and your coming in, both now and evermore. *Psalm 121*

The Minister says the words of Committal:

ALMIGHTY God, our heavenly Father, we praise you for the sure and certain hope of the resurrection to eternal life for all who trust in the Lord Jesus Christ. We now commit the ashes of N. to the ground [or to

Interment or Scattering of Ashes

their resting-place]: earth to earth, ashes to ashes, dust to dust, rejoicing that on the last day Christ will transform the bodies of all who trust in him into the likeness of his own glorious resurrection body. *Amen.*

The Minister prays for the bereaved using this or this with other prayers:

ALMIGHTY God, Father of all mercies and giver of all comfort, deal graciously, we pray, with those who mourn, and especially with the family and friends of N. gathered here so that, casting their care on you, they may know the power of your love to console them, through Jesus Christ our Lord. *Amen.*

The service ends with the Grace.

THE grace of our Lord Jesus Christ, and the love of God, and the fellowship of the Holy Spirit, be with us all evermore. *Amen.*

Daily Prayer for Use in Families

Morning Prayer

When all are gathered together, a parent invites each one present to be aware of God's presence. A scripture verse such as one of the following may be used:

New are your mercies each morning, Lord, and great is your faithfulness.

Or

Lord God, you are my God, early will I seek you. In the morning I will direct my prayer unto you, and will look up.

Let us pray.

We give you sincere thanks, heavenly Father, for the sleep and rest of the past night, and for the gift of a new day. Grant that we may so pass its hours in the perfect freedom of your service, that when evening comes we may again desire to give you thanks; through Jesus Christ our Lord. *Amen*

Then there shall be read a short passage of Scripture, possibly taken from part of the Daily Lectionary. It may be followed by a short silence before a parent says:

Let us pray.

Family Prayer

Traditional

Our Father who art in heaven, Hallowed be thy Name, Thy kingdom come, Thy will be done, on earth as it is in heaven. Give us this day our daily bread; And forgive us our trespasses, as we forgive them that trespass against us; And lead us not into temptation, but deliver us from evil. For thine is the kingdom, the power and the glory, forever and ever. Amen.

Contemporary

Our Father in heaven, hallowed be your name. Your kingdom come, your will be done, on earth as in heaven. Give us today our daily bread. Forgive us our sins as we forgive those who sin against us. Lead us not into temptation but deliver us from evil. For yours is the kingdom, and the power, and the glory, forever and ever. Amen.

Here the Collect of the Day may be used before the following prayers.

Gracious Father, we recognize that it is by your mercy that another day is added to our lives. We dedicate ourselves, souls and bodies, to you and to your service, as we begin this day as your adopted children. Confirm and strengthen us in this resolution, we pray, so that as we grow in age, we may also grow in grace and in the knowledge of our Lord and Savior Jesus Christ. *Amen.*

Heavenly Father, Almighty and Everlasting God, we thank you that you have brought us safely to the beginning of this day; defend us, your humble servants, with your mighty power and grant that we nei-

Family Prayer

ther fall into sin, nor run into any kind of danger; also grant that, being guided and governed by you, we may do what is right in your sight; through Jesus Christ our Lord. *Amen.*

Here may be included brief petitions and intercessions ending with,

Lord in your mercy, hear our prayer.

All say 2 Corinthians 13:14.

THE grace of our Lord Jesus Christ, and the love of God, and the fellowship of the Holy Spirit, be with us all evermore. *Amen.*

Evening Prayer

When all are gathered together, a parent invites each one present to be aware of God's presence. A scripture verse such as one of the following may be used:

LORD, let our prayer be set forth in your sight as the incense, and the lifting up of our hands as an evening sacrifice.

Or

THE Lord is in his holy temple; let all the earth keep silence before him.

Then there shall be read a short passage of Scripture, possibly taken from part of the Daily Lectionary. A short period of silence may follow before a parent shall say:

Let us confess our sins to Almighty God.

Family Prayer

ALMIGHTY Father, Lord of heaven and earth, we confess that we have sinned against you in thought, word, and deed. Because of your great goodness, have mercy upon us, Lord our God, through the richness of your grace take away our offences, wash us thoroughly from our wickedness, and cleanse us from all our sins; for Jesus Christ's sake. *Amen.*

Then a parent prays:

ALMIGHTY Father, you who of your great love for the world gave your only Son to die for us: Grant that through his Cross our sins may be put away and remembered no more against us, and also, cleansed by his Blood, and mindful of his sufferings, we may take up our cross daily, and follow him in newness of life, until we come to his everlasting kingdom; through the same your Son, Jesus Christ our Lord. *Amen.*

Here may follow the Collect of the Day and/or brief petitions and intercessions before the following prayers.

LORD God, you who know our every weakness, put away from us all worry and every anxious fear. Having ended the work and play of this day under your care and protection, we now commit ourselves, and all whom we love, into your gracious keeping; and as night comes, provide for us, we pray, your priceless gift of sleep; through Jesus Christ our Lord. *Amen.*

LIGHTEN our darkness, Lord, we pray, and by your great mercy defend us from all perils and dangers

Family Prayer

of this night; for the love of your only Son, our Savior Jesus Christ. *Amen.*

Here all may say together:

Traditional

OUR Father who art in heaven, Hallowed be thy Name, Thy kingdom come, Thy will be done, on earth as it is in heaven. Give us this day our daily bread; And forgive us our trespasses, as we forgive them that trespass against us; And lead us not into temptation, but deliver us from evil. For thine is the kingdom, the power and the glory, forever and ever. Amen.

Contemporary

OUR Father in heaven, hallowed be your name. Your kingdom come, your will be done, on earth as in heaven. Give us today our daily bread. Forgive us our sins as we forgive those who sin against us. Lead us not into temptation but deliver us from evil. For yours is the kingdom, and the power, and the glory, forever and ever. Amen.

WE will lie down in peace and take our rest; for it is you, Lord, only, who make us dwell in safety.

You, Lord, are in the midst of us, and we are called by your name. Do not leave us, O Lord our God.

Preserve us, Lord, waking, and guard us sleeping, that awake we may watch with Christ, and asleep we may rest in peace. Amen.

Family Prayer

Commendation

May the Lord Almighty grant us a quiet night, and at the last a perfect end; and may the blessing of God Almighty, the Father, the Son, and the Holy Spirit, be with us this night, and for evermore. *Amen.*

Grace to be said before and after meals.

Grace before a meal

Heavenly Father, bless this food for our use and us in your service; and help us to remember the needs of others; for Jesus Christ's sake. *Amen.*

The King of eternal glory make us partakers of his heavenly table. And may this food be our refreshment and God's grace be our benediction. *Amen.*

O Lord Jesus Christ, without whom nothing is sweet or savory, we humbly ask you to bless us and our meal, and with your blessed presence to cheer our hearts, that in all our meat and drink we may taste and savor you, to your honor and glory. *Amen.*

Grace after a meal

Thank you for the world so sweet,
Thank you for the food we eat.
Thank you for the birds that sing,
Thank you, God, for everything.

Blessed be God in all his gifts, and holy in all his works. Our help is in the name of the Lord, who has

Family Prayer

made both heaven and earth. Blessed be the name of our Lord, now and always, and forever. *Amen.*

Most mighty Lord and merciful Father, we offer to you sincere thanks for our bodily sustenance, and we ask you, in your gracious goodness, so to feed us with the food of your heavenly grace, that we may worthily glorify your holy Name in this life, and after it partake of the life everlasting, through our Lord Jesus Christ. *Amen.*

The Daily Lectionary

Introduction

To engage fully in Common Prayer, two Lectionaries are needed. First, there is the Eucharistic Lectionary, which is used in The Order for Holy Communion. This is printed above together with the Collects for Sundays and Holy Days. It is based upon that which is found in each of the three editions of The Book of Common Prayer, those of 1662, 1928 and 1962.

Secondly, there is the Lectionary for the Daily Office, for Morning and Evening Prayer. What is printed here is that approved by the Church of England in 1871 as a revision of the original Daily Lectionary, printed in the first editions of The Book of Common Prayer. With it, are provided the Psalms for the day based on the traditional Anglican use of the whole Psalter each month, and as the Psalter is sub-divided within The Book of Common Prayer. This 1871 form of the Lectionary is printed in most pew editions of The Book of Common Prayer (1662), published by the Presses of the Universities of Cambridge and Oxford.

For those who wish to explore the use of other Lectionaries, all they need to do is to look at those printed in the 1928 and 1962 editions of The Book of Common Prayer in North America ,and make copies of them. Also they can obtain a copy of the annual booklet "The Lectionary, CW & BCP" of the Church of England published by the SPCK of London.

For those who find that the full complement of Psalms required by the traditional Lectionary of 1871 is too much for daily meditation, there is provided in the Canadian 1962 Prayer Book a one-page Table of a much reduced daily use of the Psalter.

In the 1871 Lectionary that follows here (but not in the Eucharistic Lectionary above), when the reading starts within a chapter and goes to the end of that chapter, then it is indicated in this manner—Job 10:24 (that is, from verse 24 to the end of the chapter) and 1 John 4:7 (that is, from verse 7 to the end of the chapter).

Daily Lectionary

January		Morning Prayer			Evening Prayer		
		Psalms	1st Lesson	2nd Lesson	Psalms	1st Lesson	2nd Lesson
1	Circumcision	1 - 5	Gen. 17:9	Rom. 2:17	6 - 8	Deut. 10:12	Col.. 2:8-18
2		9 - 11	1:1-20	Matt. 1:18	12 - 14	Gen. 1:20-2:4	Acts 1
3		15 - 17	2:4	2	18	3:1-20	2:1-22
4		19 - 21	3:20-4:16	3	22 - 23	4:16	2:22
5		24 - 26	5:1-28	4:1-23	27 - 29	5:28-6:9	3
6	Epiphany	30 - 31	Isa. 60	Luke 3:15-23	32 - 34	Isa. 49:13-24	John 2:1-12
7		35 - 36	Gen. 6:9	Matt. 4:23-5:13	37	Gen. 7	Acts 4:1-32
8	Lucian, P. & M.	38 - 40	8	5:13-33	41 - 43	9:1-20	4:32-5:17
9		44 - 46	11:1-10	5:33	47 - 49	12	5:17
10		50 - 52	13	6:1-19	53 - 55	14	6
11		56 - 58	15	6:19-7:7	59 - 61	16	7:1-35
12		62 - 64	17:1-23	7:7	65 - 67	18:1-17	7:35-8:5
13	Hilary, Bp. & C.	68	18:17	8:1-18	69 - 70	19:12-30	8:5-26
14		71 - 72	20	8:18	73 - 74	21:1-22	8:26
15		75 - 77	21:33-22:20	9:1-18	78	23	9:1-23
16		79 - 81	24:1-29	9:18	82 - 85	24:29-52	9:23
17		86 - 88	24:52	10:1-24	89	25:5-19	10:1-24
18	Prisca, V. & M.	90 - 92	25:19	10:24	93 - 94	26:1-18	10:24
19		95 - 97	26:18	11	98 - 101	27:1-30	11
20	Fabian, Bp. & M.	102 - 103	27:30	12:1-22	104	28	12
21	Agnes, V. & M.	105	29:1-21	12:22	106	31:1-25	13:1-26
22	Vincent, Mart.	107	31:36	13:1-24	108 - 109	32:1-22	13:26
23		110 - 113	32:22	13:24-53	114 - 115	33	14
24		116 - 118	35:1-21	13:53-14:13	119:1-32	37:1-12	15:1-30
25	Paul, Conv.	119:33-72	Isa. 49:1-13	Gal. 1:11	119:73-104	Jer. 1:1-11	26:1-21
26		119:105-144	Gen. 37:12	Matt. 14:13	119:145-176	Gen. 39	15:30-16:16
27		120 - 125	40	15:1-21	126 - 131	41:1-17	16:16
28		132 - 135	41:17-53	15:21	136 - 138	41:53-42:25	17:1-16
29		139 - 141	42:25	16:1-24	142 - 143	43:1-25	17:16
30		144 - 146	43:25-44:14	16:24-17:14	147 - 150	44:14	18:1-24
31		144 - 146	45:1-25	17:14	147 - 150	45:25-46:8	18:24-19:21

Daily Lectionary

February		Morning Prayer			Evening Prayer		
		Psalms	1st Lesson	2nd Lesson	Psalms	1st Lesson	2nd Lesson
1	Fast.	1 - 5	Gen. 46:26-47:13	Matt. 18:1-21	6 - 8	Gen. 47:13	Acts 19:21
2	Presentation	9 - 11	Ex. 13:11-16	18:21-19:3	12 - 14	Hag. 2:1-10	20:1-17
3		15 - 17	48	19:3-27	18	49	20:17
4		19 - 21	50	19:27-20:17	22 - 23	Ex. 1	21:1-17
5	Agatha, V. & M.	24 - 26	Ex. 2	20:17	27 - 29	3	21:17-37
6		30 - 31	4:1-24	21:1-23	32 - 34	4:27-5:15	21:37-22:23
7		35 - 36	5:15-6:14	21:23	37	6:28-7:14	22:23-23:12
8		38 - 40	7:14	22:1-15	41 - 43	8:1-20	23:12
9		44 - 46	8:20-9:13	22:15-41	47 - 49	9:13	24
10		50 - 52	10:1-21	22:41-23:13	53 - 55	10:21 & 11	25
11		56 - 58	12:1-21	23:13	59 - 61	12:21-43	26
12		62 - 64	12:43-13:17	24:1-29	65 - 67	13:17-14:10	27:1-18
13		68	14:10	24:29	69 - 70	15:1-22	27:18
14	Valentine, Bishop	71 - 72	15:22-16:11	25:1-31	73 - 74	16:11	28:1-17
15		75 - 77	17	25:31	78	18	28:17
16		79 - 81	19	26:1-31	82 - 85	20:1-22	Rom. 1
17		86 - 88	21:1-18	26:31-57	89	22:21-23:10	2:1-17
18		90 - 92	23:14	26:57	93 - 94	24	2:17
19		95 - 97	25:1-23	27:1-27	98 - 101	28:1-13	3
20		102 - 103	28:29-42	27:27-57	104	29:35-30:11	4
21		105	31	27:57	106	32:1-15	5
22		107	32:15	28	108 - 109	33:1-12	6
23	Fast	110 - 113	33:12-34:10	Mark 1:1-21	114 - 115	34:10-27	7
24	Matthias, Ap.	116 - 118	1 Sam. 2:27-36	1:21	119:1-32	Isa. 22:15	8:1-18
25		119:33-72	34:27	2:1-23	119:73-104	35:29-36:8	8:18
26		119:105-144	39:30	2:23-3:13	119:145-176	40:1-17	9:1-19
27		120 - 125	40:17	3:13	126 - 131	Lev. 9:22-10:12	9:19
28		132 - 135	Lev. 14:1-23	4:1-35	136 - 138	16:1-23	10
29		139 - 141	19:1-19	7	142 - 143	19:30-20:9	12

Daily Lectionary

March		Morning Prayer			Evening Prayer		
		Psalms	1st Lesson	2nd Lesson	Psalms	1st Lesson	2nd Lesson
1	David, Archbp.	1 - 5	Lev. 25:1-18	Mark 4:35-5:21	6 - 8	Lev. 25:18-44	Rom. 11:1-25
2	Chad, Bishop	9 - 11	26:1-21	5:21	12 - 14	26:21	11:25
3		15 - 17	Num. 6	6:1-14	18	Num. 9:15-10:11	12
4		19 – 21	10:11	6:14-30	22 – 23	11:1-24	13
5		24 – 26	11:24	6:30	27 – 29	12	14-15:8
6		30 – 31	13:17	7:1-24	32 – 34	14:1-26	15:8
7	Perpetua, M.	35 – 36	14:26	7:24-8:10	37	16:1-23	16
8		38 – 40	16:23	8:10-9:2	41 – 43	17	1 Cor. 1:1-26
9		44 – 46	20:1-14	9:2:1-30	47 – 49	20:14	1:26 & 2
10		50 – 52	21:1-10	9:30	53 – 55	21:10-32	3
11		56 – 58	22:1-22	10:1-32	59 – 61	22:22	4:1-18
12	Gregory, M. B.	62 - 64	23	10:32	65 – 67	24	4:18 & 5
13		68	25	11:1-27	69 – 70	27:12	6
14		71 – 72	Deuter. 1:1-19	11:27-12:13	73 – 74	Deuter. 1:19	7:1-25
15		75 – 77	2:1-26	12:13-35	78	2:26-3:18	7:25
16		79 – 81	3:18	12:35-13:14	82 – 85	4:1-25	8
17		86 – 88	4:25-41	13:14	89	5:1-22	9
18	Edward, King	90 – 92	5:22	14:1-27	93 – 94	6	10 & 11:1
19		95 – 97	7:1-12	14:27-53	98 – 101	7:12	11:2-17
20		102 – 103	8	14:53	104	10:8	11:17
21	Benedict, Abbot.	105	11:1-18	15:1-42	106	11:18	12:1-28
22		107	15:1-16	15:42 & 16	108 – 109	17:8	12:28 & 13
23		110 – 113	18:9	Luke 1:1-26	114 – 115	24:5	14:1-20
24	Fast	116 – 118	26	1:26-46	119:1-32	27	14:20
25	Annunciation	119:33-72	Gen. 3:1-16	1:46	119:73-104	Isa. 52:7-13	15:1-35
26		119:105-144	Deuter. 28:1-15	2:1-21	119:145-176	Deuter. 28:15-47	15:35
27		120 – 125	28:47	2:21	126 – 131	29:9	16
28		132 – 135	30	3:1-23	136 – 138	31:1-14	2 Cor. 1:1-23
29		139 – 141	31:14-30	4:1-16	142 – 143	31:30-32:44	1:23-2:14
30		144 – 146	32:44	4:16	147 – 150	33	2:14 & 3
31		144 – 146	34	5:1-17	147 – 150	Josh. 1	4

Daily Lectionary

April		Morning Prayer			Evening Prayer		
		Psalms	1st Lesson	2nd Lesson	Psalms	1st Lesson	2nd Lesson
1		1 - 5	Josh. 2	Luke 5:17	6 - 8	Josh. 3	2 Cor. 5
2		9 – 11	4	6:1-20	12 – 14	5	6 & 7:1
3	Richard, Bp.	15 – 17	6	6:20	18	7	7:2
4	S. Ambrose, Bp.	19 – 21	9:3	7:1-24	22 – 23	10:1-16	8
5		24 – 26	21:43-22:11	7:24	27 – 29	22:11	9
6		30 – 31	23	8:1-26	32 – 34	24	10
7		35 – 36	Judges 2	8:26	37	Judges 4	11:1-30
8		38 – 40	5	9:1-28	41 – 43	6:1-24	11:30-12:14
9		44 – 46	6:24	9:28-51	47 – 49	7	12:14 & 13
10		50 – 52	8:32-9:25	9:51-10:17	53 – 55	10	Gal. 1
11		56 – 58	11:1-29	10:17	59 – 61	11:29	2
12		62 – 64	13	11:1-29	65 – 67	14	3
13		68	15	11:29	69 – 70	16	4:1-21
14		71 – 72	Ruth 1	12:1-35	73 – 74	Ruth 2	4:21-5:13
15		75 – 77	3	12:35	78	4	5:13
16		79 – 81	1 Sam. 1	13:1-18	82 – 85	1 Sam. 1-21	6
17		86 – 88	2:21	13:18	89	3	Eph. 1
18		90 – 92	4	14:1-25	93 – 94	5	2
19	Alphege, Abp.	95 – 97	6	14:25-15:11	98 – 101	7	3
20		102 – 103	8	15:11	104	9	4:1-25
21		105	10	16	106	11	4:25-5:22
22		107	12	17:1-20	108 – 109	13	5:22-6:10
23	St. George, M.	110 – 113	14:1-24	17:20	114 – 115	14:24-47	6:10
24		116 – 118	15	18:1-31	119:1-32	16	Phil. 1
25	Mark, Evang.	119:33-72	Isa. 62:6	18:31-19:11	119:73-104	Eze. 1:1-15	2
26		119:105-144	1 Sam. 17:1-31	19:11-28	119:145-176	1 Sam. 17:31-55	3
27		120 – 125	17:55-18:17	19:28	126 – 131	19	4
28		132 – 135	20:1-18	20:1-27	136 – 138	20:18	Col. 1:1-21
29		139 – 141	21	20:27-21:5	142 – 143	22	1:21-2:8
30		144 – 146	23	21:5	147 – 150	24 & 25:1	2:8

Daily Lectionary

May		Morning Prayer			Evening Prayer		
		Psalms	1st Lesson	2nd Lesson	Psalms	1st Lesson	1st Lesson
1	Philip & James,	1 – 5	Isa. 61	John 1:43	6 – 8	Zech. 4	Col. 3:1-18
2		9 – 11	1 Sam. 26	Luke 22:1-31	12 – 14	1 Sam. 28:3	3:18-4:7
3	Invent. of Cross	15 – 17	31	22:31-54	18	2 Sam. 1	4:7
4		19 – 21	2 Sam. 3:17	22:54	22 – 23	4	1 Thess. 1
5		24 – 26	6	23:1-26	27 – 29	7:1-18	2
6	St. John, E. ante Port. Lat.	30 – 31	7:18	23:26-50	32 – 34	9	3
7		35 – 36	11	23:50-24:13	37	12:1-24	4
8		38 – 40	13:38-14:26	24:13	41 – 43	15:1-16	5
9		44 – 46	15:16	John 1:1-29	47 – 49	16:1-15	2 Thess. 1
10		50 – 52	16:15-17:24	1:29	53 – 55	17:24-18:18	2
11		56 – 58	18:18	2	59 – 61	19:1-24	3
12		62 – 64	19:24	3:1-22	65 – 67	21:1-15	1 Tim. 1:1-18
13		68	23:1-24	3:22	69 – 70	24	1:18-20 & 2
14		71 – 72	1 Kings 1:1-28	4:1-31	73 – 74	1 Kgs 1:28-49	3
15		75 – 77	1 Chron. 29:10	4:31	78	3	4
16		79 – 81	1 Kings 4:20	5:1-24	82 – 85	5	5
17		86 – 88	6:1-15	5:24	89	8:1-22	6
18		90 – 92	8:22-54	6:1-22	93 – 94	8:54-9:10	2 Tim. 1
19	Dunstan, Archbp.	95 – 97	10	6:22-41	98 – 101	11:1-26	2
20		102 – 103	11:26	6:41	104	12:1-25	3
21		105	12:25-13:11	7:1-25	106	13:11	4
22		107	14:1-21	7:25	108 – 109	15:25-16:8	Titus 1
23		110 – 113	16:8	8:1-31	114 – 115	17	2
24		116 – 118	18:1-17	8:31	119:1-32	18:17	3
25		119:33-72	19	9:1-39	119:73-104	21	Philemon
26	Augustine, Archbp.	119:105-144	22:1-41	9:39-10:22	119:145-176	2 Kings 1	Heb. 1
27	Ven. Bede, Presb.	120 – 125	2 Kings 2	10:22	126 – 131	4:8	2 & 3:1-7
28		132 – 135	5	11:1-17	136 – 138	6:1-24	3:7-4:14
29		139 – 141	6:24	11:17-47	142 – 143	7	4:14 & 5
30		144 – 146	8:1-16	11:47-12:20	147 – 150	9	6
31		144 – 146	10:1-18	12:20	147 - 150	10:18	7

Daily Lectionary

June		Morning Prayer			Evening Prayer		
		Psalms	1st Lesson	2nd Lesson	Psalms	1st Lesson	2nd Lesson
1	Nicomede, M.	1 – 5	2 Kings 13	John 13:1-21	6 – 8	2 Kings 17:1-24	Heb. 8
2		9 – 11	17:24	13:21	12 – 14	2 Chron. 12	9
3		15 – 17	2 Chron. 13	14	18	14	10:1-19
4		19 – 21	15	15	22 – 23	16 & 17:1-14	10:19
5	Boniface, Bishop.	24 – 26	19	16:1-16	27 – 29	20:1-31	11:1-17
6		30 – 31	20:31 & 21	16:16	32 – 34	22	11:17
7		35 – 36	23	17	37	24	12
8		38 – 40	25	18:1-28	41 – 43	26 & 27	13
9		44 – 46	28	18:28	47 – 49	2 Kings 18:1-9	James 1
10		50 – 52	29:3-21	19:1-25	53 – 55	2 Chr.30 & 31:1	2
11	Barnabas, Ap.	56 – 58	Deut. 33:1-12	Acts 4:31	59 – 61	Nahum 1	Acts 14:8
12		62 – 64	2 Kings 18:13	19:25	65 – 67	2 Kings 19:1-20	James 3
13		68	19:20	20:1-19	69 – 70	20	4
14		71 – 72	Isa. 38:9-21	20:19	73 – 74	2 Chron. 33	5
15		75 – 77	2 Kings 22	21	78	2 Kings 23:1-21	1 Peter 1:1-22
16		79 – 81	23:21-24:8	Acts 1	82 – 85	24:8-25:8	1:22-2:11
17	St. Alban, Mart.	86 – 88	25:8	2:1-22	89	Ezra 1 & 3	2:11-3:8
18		90 – 92	Ezra 4	2:22	93 – 94	5	3:8-4:7
19		95 – 97	7	3	98 – 101	8:15	4:7
20	Tr. of King Edw.	102 – 103	9	4:1-32	104	10:1-20	5
21		105	Neh. 1	4:32-5:17	106	Neh. 2	2 Peter 1
22		107	4	5:17	108 – 109	5	2
23	Fast	110 – 113	6 & 7:1-5	6	114 – 115	7:73 & 8	3
24	John Baptist	116 - 118	Mal. 3:1-7	Matt. 3	119:1-32	Mal. 4	Matt. 14:1-13
25		119:33-72	Neh. 13:1-15	Acts 7:1-35	119:73-104	Neh. 13:15	1 John 1
26		119:105-144	Esther 1	7:35-8:5	119:145-176	Est. 2:15 & 3	2:1-15
27		120 – 125	4	8:5-26	126 – 131	5	2:15
28	Fast.	132 – 135	6	8:26	136 – 138	7	3:1-16
29	Peter, Apostle	139 – 141	Eze. 3:4-15	John 21:15-23	142 – 143	Zech. 3	Acts 4:8-23
30		144 – 146	Job 1	Acts 9:1-23	147 – 150	Job 2	1 Jo. 3:16-4:7

Daily Lectionary

July		Morning Prayer			Evening Prayer		
		Psalms	1st Lesson	2nd Lesson	Psalms	1st Lesson	2nd Lesson
1		1 – 5	Job 3	Acts 9:23	6 – 8	Job 4	1 John 4:7
2	Visitation of the Blessed Virgin Mary	9 – 11	5	10:1-24	12 – 14	6	5
3		15 – 17	7	10:24	18	9	2 John
4	Tr. of St. Martin	19 – 21	10	11	22 – 23	11	3 John
5		24 – 26	12	12	27 – 29	13	Jude
6		30 – 31	14	13:1-26	32 – 34	16	Matt. 1:18
7		35 – 36	17	13:26	37	19	2
8		38 – 40	21	14	41 – 43	22:12-29	3
9		44 – 46	23	15:1-30	47 – 49	24	4:1-23
10		50 – 52	25 & 26	15:30-16:16	53 – 55	27	4:23-5:13
11		56 – 58	28	16:16	59 – 61	29 & 30:1	5:13-33
12		62 – 64	30:12-27	17:1-16	65 – 67	31:13	5:33
13		68	32	17:16	69 – 70	38:1-39	6:1-19
14		72 – 72	38:39 & 39	18:1-24	73 – 74	40	6:19-7:7
15	Swithun, Bishop	75 – 77	41	18:24-19:21	78	42	7:7
16		79 – 81	Prov. 1:1-20	19:21	82 – 85	Prov. 1:20	8:1-18
17		86 – 88	2	20:1-17	89	3:1-27	8:18
18		90 – 92	3:27-4:20	20:17	93 – 94	4:20-5:15	9:1-18
19		95 – 97	5:15	21:1-17	98 – 101	6:1-20	9:18
20	Margaret V. & M.	102 – 103	7	21:17-37	104	8	10:1-24
21		105	9	21:37-22:23	106	10:16	10:24
22	Mary Magdalen	107	11:1-15	22:23-23:12	108 – 109	11:15	11
23		110 – 113	12:10	23:12	114 – 115	13	12:1-22
24	Fast.	116 – 118	14:9-28	24	119:1-32	14:28-15:18	12:22
25	James, Apostle	119:33-72	2 Kings 1:1-16	Luke 9:51-57	119:73-104	Jer. 26:8-16	13:1-24
26	St. Anne	119:105-144	Prov. 15:18	Acts 25	119:145-176	Prov. 16:1-20	13:24-53
27		120 – 125	16:31-17:18	26	126 – 131	18:10	13:53-14:13
28		132 – 135	19:13	27	136 – 138	20:1-23	14:13
29		139 – 141	21:1-17	28:1-17	142 – 143	22:1-17	15:1-21
30		144 – 146	23:10	28:17	147 – 150	24:21	15:21
31		144 – 146	25	Rom. 1	147 - 150	26:1-21	16:1-24

Daily Lectionary

August		Morning Prayer			Evening Prayer		
		Psalms	1st Lesson	2nd Lesson	Psalms	1st Lesson	2nd Lesson
1	Lammas Day	1 – 5	Prov. 27:1-23	Rom. 2:1-17	6 – 8	Prov. 28:1-15	Matt. 16:24-17:14
2		9 – 11	30:1-18	2:17	12 – 14	31:10	17:14
3		15 – 17	Eccl. 1	3	18	Eccl. 2:1-12	18:1-21
4		19 – 21	3	4	22 – 23	4	18:21-19:3
5		24 – 26	5	5	27 – 29	6	19:3-27
6	Transfiguration	30 – 31	7	6	32 – 34	8	19:27-20:17
7	Name of Jesus	35 – 36	9	7	37	11	20:17
8		38 – 40	12	8:1-18	41 – 43	Jer. 1	21:1-23
9		44 – 46	Jer. 2:1-14	8:18	47 – 49	5:1-19	21:23
10	St. Lawrence, M.	50 – 52	5:19	9:1-19	53 – 55	6:1-22	22:1-15
11		56 – 58	Jer. 7:1-17	9:19	59 – 61	8:4	22:15-41
12		62 – 64	9:1-17	10	65 – 67	13:8-24	22:41-23:13
13		68	15	11:1-25	69 – 70	17:1-19	23:13
14		71 – 72	18:1-18	11:25	73 – 74	19	24:1-29
15		75 – 77	21	12	78	22:1-13	24:29
16		79 – 81	22:13	13	82 – 85	23:1-16	25:1-31
17		86 – 88	24	14 & 15:1-8	89	25:1-15	25:31
18		90 – 92	26	15:8	93 – 94	28	26:1-31
19		95 – 97	29:4-20	16	98 – 101	30	26:31-57
20		102 – 103	31:1-15	1 Cor. 1:1-26	104	31:15-38	26:57
21		105	33:1-14	1:26 & 2	106	33:14	27:1-27
22		107	35	3	108 – 109	36:1-14	27:27-57
23	Fast.	110 – 113	36:14	4:1-18	114 – 115	38:1-14	27:57
24	Bartholomew	116 – 118	Gen. 28:10-18	4:18 & 5	119:1-32	Deuter. 18:15	28
25		119:33-72	Jerem. 38:14	6	119:73-104	Jerem. 39	Mark 1:1-21
26		119:105-144	50:1-21	7:1-25	119:145-176	51:54	1:21
27		120 – 125	Eze. 1:1-15	7:25	126 – 131	Eze. 1:15	2:1-23
28	St. Augustine, B.	132 – 135	2	8	136 – 138	3:1-15	2:23-3:13
29	Beheading of St. John Baptist	139 – 141	3:15	9	142 – 143	8	3:13
30		144 – 146	9	10 & 11:1	147 – 150	11:14	4:1-35
31		144 – 146	12:17	11:2-17	147 – 150	13:1-17	4:35-5:21

Daily Lectionary

September		Morning Prayer			Evening Prayer		
		Psalms	1st Lesson	2nd Lesson	Psalms	1st Lesson	2nd Lesson
1	Giles, Abbot.	1 – 5	Eze. 13:17	1 Cor. 11:17	6 – 8	Eze. 14:1-12	Mark 5:21
2		9 – 11	14:12	12:1-28	12 – 14	16:44	6:1-14
3		15 – 17	18:1-19	12:28 & 13	18	18:19	6:14-30
4		19 – 21	20:1-18	14:1-20	22 – 23	20:18-33	6:30
5		24 – 26	20:33-44	14:20	27 – 29	22:23	7:1-24
6		30 – 31	24:15	15:1-35	32 – 34	26	7:24-8:10
7	Enurchus, Bishop	35 – 36	27:1-26	15:35	37	27:26	8:10-9:2
8	Nat. of Vir. Mary	38 – 40	28:1-20	16	41 – 43	31	9:2-30
9		44 – 46	32:1-17	2 Cor. 1:1-23	47 – 49	33:1-21	9:30
10		50 – 52	33:21	1:23-2:14	53 – 55	34:1-17	10:1-32
11		56 – 58	34:17	2:14 & 3	59 – 61	36:16-33	10:32
12		62 – 64	37:1-15	4	65 – 67	37:15	11:1-27
13		68	47:1-13	5	69 – 70	Daniel 1	11:27-12:13
14	Holy-Cross Day	71 – 72	Daniel 2:1-24	6 & 7:1	73 – 74	2:24	12:13-35
15		75 – 77	3	7:2	78	4:1-19	12:35-13:14
16		79 – 81	4:19	8	82 – 85	5:1-17	13:14
17	Lambert, Bishop	86 – 88	5:17	9	89	6	14:1-27
18		90 – 92	7:1-15	10	93 – 94	7:15	14:27-53
19		95 – 97	9:1-20	11:1-30	98 – 101	9:20	14:53
20	Fast.	102 – 103	10:1-20	11:30-12:14	104	12	15:1-42
21	Matt., Ap.	105	1 Kings 19:15	12:14 & 13	106	1 Chr. 29:1-20	15:42 & 16
22		107	Hosea 2:14	Gal. 1	108 – 109	Hosea 4:1-13	Luke 1:1-26
23		110 – 113	5:8-6:7	2	114 – 115	7:8	1:26-57
24		116 – 118	8	3	119:1-32	9	1:57
25		119:33-72	10	4:1-21	119:73-104	11 & 12:1-7	2:1-21
26	St. Cyprian, Abp.	119:105-144	13:1-15	4:21-5:13	119:145-176	14	2:21
27		120 – 125	Joel 1	5:13	126 – 131	Joel 2:1-15	3:1-23
28		132 – 135	2:15-28	6	136 – 138	2:28-3:9	4:1-16
29	Michael & Angels	139 – 141	Gen. 32	Acts 12:5-18	142 – 143	Daniel 10:4	Rev.14:14
30	St. Jerome	144 – 146	Joel 3:9	Eph. 1	147 – 150	Amos 1 & 2:1-4	Luke 4:16

Daily Lectionary

October		Morning Prayer			Evening Prayer		
		Psalms	1st Lesson	2nd Lesson	Psalms	1st Lesson	2nd Lesson
1	Remigius, Bp.	1 – 5	Amos 2:4-3:9	Eph. 2	6 – 8	Amos 4:4	Luke 5:1-17
2		9 – 11	5:1-18	3	12 – 14	5:18-6:9	5:17
3		15 – 17	7	4:1-25	18	8	6:1-20
4		19 – 21	9	4:25-5:22	22 – 23	Obadiah	6:20
5		24 – 26	Jonah 1	5:22-6:10	27 – 29	Jonah 2	7:1-24
6	Faith, V. & M.	30 – 31	3	6:10	32 – 43	4	7:24
7		35 – 36	Micah 1:1-10	Phil. 1	37	Micah 2	8:1-26
8		38 – 40	3	2	41 – 43	4	8:26
9	St. Denys, Bishop	44 – 46	5	3	47 – 49	6	9:1-28
10		50 – 52	7	4	53 – 55	Nahum 1	9:28-51
11		56 – 58	Nahum 2	Col. 1:1-21	59 – 61	3	9:51-10:17
12		62 – 64	Habakkuk 1	1:21-2:8	65 – 67	Habakkuk 2	10:17
13	Trans. K. Edw.	68	3	2:8	69 – 70	Zeph.1:1-14	11:1-29
14		71 – 72	Zeph. 1:14-2:4	3:1-18	73 – 74	Zeph. 2:4	11:29
15		75 – 77	3	3:18 & 4	78	Hag. 1	12:1-35
16		79 – 81	Hag. 2:1-10	1 Thess 1	82 – 85	Hag. 2:10	12:35
17	Etheldreda, V.	86 – 88	Zech. 1:1-18	2	89	Zech. 1:18 & 2	13:1-18
18	Luke, Evang.	90 – 92	Isa. 55	3	93 – 94	38:1-15	13:18
19		95 – 97	Zech. 3	4	98 – 101	4	14:1-25
20		102 – 103	5	5	104	6	14:25-15:11
21		105	7	2 Thess. 1	106	8:1-14	15:11
22		107	8:14	2	108 – 109	9:9	16
23		110 – 113	10	3	114 – 115	11	17:1-20
24		116 – 118	12	1 Tim 1:1-18	119:1-32	13	17:20
25	Crispin, Martyr	119:33-72	14	1:18 & 2	119:73-104	Mal. 1	18:1-31
26		119:105-144	Mal. 2	3	119:145-176	3:1-13	18:31-19:11
27	Fast	120 – 125	3:13 & 4	4	126 – 131	Wisdom 1	19:11-28
28	Simon & Jude	132 – 135	Isa. 28:9-17	5	136 – 138	Jer. 3:12-19	19:28
29		139 – 141	Wisdom 2	6	142 – 143	Wisdom 4:7	20:1-27
30		144 – 146	6:1-22	2 Tim. 1	147 – 150	6:22-7:15	20:27-21:5
31	Fast	144 - 146	7:15	2	147 – 150	8:1-19	21:5

Daily Lectionary

November		Morning Prayer			Evening Prayer		
		Psalms	1st Lesson	2nd Lesson	Psalms	1st Lesson	2nd Lesson
1	All Saints' Day	1 – 5	Wisdom 3:1-10	Heb. 11:33-12:7	6 – 8	Wisdom 5:1-17	Rev. 19:1-17
2		9 – 11	9	2 Tim 3	12 – 14	11:1-15	Luke 22:1-31
3		15 – 17	11:15-12:3	4	18	17	22:31-54
4		19 – 21	Ecclus. 1:1-14	Titus 1	22 – 23	Ecclus. 2	22:54
5		24 – 26	3:17-30	2	27 – 29	4:10	23:1-26
6	Leonard, Conf.	30 – 31	5	3	32 – 34	7:27	23:26-50
7		35 – 36	10:18	Philemon	37	14:1-20	23:50-24:13
8		38 – 40	15:9	Heb. 1	41 – 43	16:17	24:13
9		44 – 46	18:1-15	2 & 3:1-7	47 – 49	18:15	John 1:1-29
10		50 – 52	19:13	3:7-4:14	53 – 55	22:6-24	1:29
11	St. Martin, Bp.	56 – 58	24:1-24	4:14 & 5	59 – 61	24:24	2
12		62 – 64	33:7-23	6	65 – 67	34:15	3:1-22
13	Britius, Bishop	68	35	7	69 – 70	37:8-19	3:22
14		71 – 72	39:1-13	8	73 – 74	39:13	4:1-31
15	Machutus, Bp.	75 – 77	41:1-14	9	78	42:15	4:31
16		79 – 81	44:1-16	10:1-19	82 – 85	50:1-25	5:1-24
17	Hugh, Bishop	86 – 88	51:10	10:19	89	Baruch 4:1-21	5:24
18		90 – 92	Baruch 4:36 & 5	11:1-17	93 – 94	Isa. 1:1-21	6:1-22
19		95 – 97	Isa. 1:21	11:17	98 – 101	2	6:22-41
20	Edmund, King	102 – 103	3:1-16	12	104	4:2	6:41
21		105	5:1-18	13	106	5:18	7:1-25
22	Cecilia, V. & M.	107	6	James 1	108 – 109	7:1-17	7:25
23	St. Clement, Bp.	110 – 113	8:5-18	2	114 – 115	8:18-9:8	8:1-31
24		116 – 118	9:8-10:5	3	119:1-32	10:5-20	8:31
25	Catherine, V. & M.	119:33-72	10:20	4	119:73-104	11:1-10	9:1-39
26		119:105-144	11:10	5	119:145-176	12	9:39-10:22
27		120 – 125	13	1 Peter 1:1-22	126 – 131	14:1-24	10:22
28		132 – 135	17	1:22-2:11	136 – 138	18	11:1-17
29	Fast	139 – 141	19:1-16	2:11-3:8	142 – 143	19:16	11:17-47
30	Andrew, Apostle	144 – 146	Isa. 54	John 1:35-43	147 – 150	Isa. 65:1-17	12:20-42

Daily Lectionary

December		Morning Prayer			Evening Prayer		
		Psalms	1st Lesson	2nd Lesson	Psalms	1st Lesson	2nd Lesson
1		1 - 5	Isa. 21:1-13	1 Peter 3:8-4:7	6 - 8	Isa. 22:1-15	John 11:47-12:20
2		9 - 11	22:15	4:7	12 - 14	23	12:20
3		15 - 17	24	5	18	25	13:1-21
4		19 - 21	26:1-20	2 Peter 1	22 - 23	26:20 & 27	13:21
5		24 - 26	28:1-14	2	27 - 29	28:14	14
6	Nicolas, Bishop	30 - 31	29:1-9	3	32 - 34	29:9	15
7		35 - 36	30:1-18	1 John 1	37	30:18	16:1-16
8	Conception of Virgin Mary	38 - 40	31	2:1-15	41 - 43	32	16:16
9		44 -46	33	2:15	47 - 49	34	17
10		50 - 52	35	3:1-16	53 - 55	40:1-12	18:1-28
11		56 - 58	40:12	3:16-4:7	59 - 61	41:1-17	18:28
12		62 - 64	41:17	4:7	65 - 67	42:1-18	19:1-25
13	Lucy, Virgin & Martyr	68	42:18-43:8	5	69 - 70	43:8	19:25
14		71 - 72	44:1-21	2 John	73 - 74	44:21-45:8	20:1-19
15		75 - 77	45:8	3 John	78	46	20:19
16	O Sapientia	79 - 81	47	Jude	82 - 85	48	21
17		86 - 88	49:1-13	Rev. 1	89	49:13	Rev. 2:1-18
18		90 - 92	50	2:18-3:7	93 - 94	51:1-9	3:7
19		95 - 97	51:9	4	98 - 101	52:1-13	5
20	Fast	102 - 103	52:13 & 53	6	104	54	7
21	Thomas, Ap.	105	Job 42:1-7	John 20:19-24	106	Isa. 35	John 14:1-8
22		107	Isa. 55	Revelation 8	108 - 109	56	Revelation 10
23		110 - 113	57	11	114, 115	58	12
24	Fast	116 - 118	59	14	119:1-32	60	15
25	Christmas Day	19, 45, 85	9:1-8	Luke 2:1-15	89, 110, 132	7:10-17	Titus 3:4-9
26	Stephen, Martyr	119:105-144	Gen. 4:1-11	Acts 6	119:145-176	2 Chron. 24:15-23	Acts 8:1-9
27	John, Evangelist	120 - 125	Ex. 33:9	John 13:23-36	126 - 131	Isa. 6	Revelation 1
28	Holy Innocents	132 - 135	Jer. 31:1-18	Revelation 16	136 - 138	Baruch 4:21-31	18
29		139 - 141	Isa. 61	19:1-11	142 - 143	Isa. 62	19:11
30		144 - 146	63	20	147 - 150	64 & 65:1-8	21:1-15
31	Silvester, Bishop	144 - 146	65:8	21:15-22:6	147 - 150	66	22:6

The Ordinal
*The Form and Manner of Making Deacons,
Ordaining of Priests and
Consecrating of Bishops in the Church of God*

Introduction

The essentials in ordination are "the form" and "the manner:" and these point to Prayer by clergy and people, and the Laying on of hands primarily by the Bishop.

The original text of these services assumes that there will be several or many candidates for the diaconate and priesthood, but only one for the episcopate. On occasions through the centuries since 1550, and particularly in more recent times, there have been single ordinations to the diaconate and priesthood and several to the episcopate.

Making deacons, and ordaining priests, at the "center" of the settled or missionary diocese places emphasis upon the Bishop as the focus of unity; in contrast, the going of the Bishop to the local church or mission center to make a deacon, or ordain a priest, helps the laity appreciate the meaning of ordained ministry.

In general, a useful distinction is between the act of ordination to any of the three Orders, and the reception of the individual person ordained at his sphere of service. The two have usually been distinct, for they do relate to two different things, both necessary.

The Preface

IT is clear to all who diligently read Holy Scripture and study the writings of the ancient Fathers, that from the apostolic age there have been three Orders of Ministers in the Church of Christ – Bishops, Presbyters (Priests) and Deacons. These offices were always held in such high esteem that no person might presume to

The Ordinal

perform any of them, except he were first called, tested, examined, and known to have such qualities as are required for them; and also, in a public Service, with the laying on of hands, were approved and admitted by lawful authority into them.

Therefore, to the intent that these three Orders may be continued, reverently used and esteemed in this Church, it is required that no man shall be accepted and received as a lawful Bishop, Priest or Deacon, and allowed to perform any ministerial function attached to the office, unless he is first called, tested and examined, and admitted into the office, according to the Form that follows or unless he has already received Episcopal Consecration or Ordination.

The Form and Manner of Making of Deacons

On the appointed day, the Service begins with Morning Prayer, which is followed immediately by a Sermon or Exhortation, in which the office and duty of those who are to be made deacons are declared, the necessity of the office of Deacon in the Church of Christ explained, and how the people of God ought to regard those who are made Deacons, stated. After the Sermon or Exhortation, a senior Minister presents to the Bishop (who is sitting in his Chair near to the holy Table) those who are candidates for ordination, and who are appropriately robed for the occasion.

REVEREND Father in God, I present unto you these persons here present to be admitted as Deacons in the Church of Christ.

The Bishop,

HAVE you made sure that these persons, whom you present to us, are truly suited and prepared, by their knowledge of Holy Scripture, sound doctrine and holiness of life, to exercise their ministry in due time and manner to the glory of God and the building up of his Church?

A senior Minister replies,

I HAVE examined them and I believe that they are suited and prepared for this Ministry.

The Bishop addresses the congregation:

BROTHERS and Sisters in Christ, if any of you knows a good reason why any of these persons should not

The Making of Deacons

be admitted to the office of Deacon, come forward in the Name of God, and make known that reason.

> If any serious objection is alleged against a candidate, the Bishop shall postpone that person's ordination so that proper investigation can be made.
>
> The Bishop proceeds by commending to the prayers of the congregation all those against whom no objection has been lodged. Thus here shall be said or sung the Litany, adding this Suffrage: **To bless these your servants who are to be admitted to the Office of Deacon, and to pour your grace upon them; that they may in due time exercise their office to the edifying of your Church, and to the glory of your holy Name.** After the Litany, the Service of Holy Communion begins with this Collect, followed by the Epistle.

ALMIGHTY God, you who by your divine providence have appointed various Orders of Ministers in your Church, and who inspired your apostles to choose for the Order of Deacons the first martyr Saint Stephen with others: Look in mercy on these your servants also called to the office of Deacon; so replenish them with the truth of your teaching, and adorn them with holiness of life, that, both by word and good example, they may faithfully serve you in this office, to the glory of your Name, and the building up of your Church; through the merits of our Savior Jesus Christ, who lives and reigns with you and the Holy Spirit, now and forever. *Amen.*

The Epistle: 1 Timothy 3:8–13 or Acts 6:2–7

> Before the Gospel, the Bishop examines the candidates.

The Making of Deacons

Do you trust that you are inwardly moved by the Holy Spirit to undertake this office and ministry, and to serve God by the promoting of his glory, and the building up of his people?
Answer. I trust that I am so moved.

Do you think that you are truly called, according to the will of our Lord Jesus Christ, and the Order of this Church, to the Ministry of the Church?
Answer. I think that I am so called.

Are you convinced that the Holy Scriptures contain sufficiently all doctrine necessarily required for eternal salvation through faith in Jesus Christ?
Answer. I am convinced of this.

Will you diligently read these Scriptures to the people assembled in the Church where you will be appointed to serve?
Answer. I will do so.

It belongs to the office of a Deacon, in the Church where appointed to serve, to assist the Priest in Divine Service, and especially when he administers the Holy Communion. Also the Deacon publicly reads the Scriptures, instructs the youth in the content of the Faith, conducts the service of Holy Baptism when asked, and preaches, if licensed to do so by the Bishop. In addition, the Deacon is called to work with church members in caring for the sick and needy in the congregation and local community. Will you gladly and willingly do this?

The Making of Deacons

Answer. I will do so, with God's help.

WILL you diligently seek to order your own lives, and that of your families, in such a way that you follow the teaching of Christ, and are thereby, to the greatest degree possible, wholesome examples to the flock of Christ?
Answer. I will do so, the Lord being my helper.

WILL you reverently obey the Ministers who are set over you in authority in the Church, and will you gladly and readily follow their godly advice?
Answer. I will do so, the Lord being my helper.

Then, as each candidate kneels humbly before him, the Bishop lays his hands upon his head and says,

TAKE authority to exercise the office of a Deacon in the Church of God, now committed to you, in the Name of the Father, and of the Son, and of the Holy Spirit. *Amen.*

Then the Bishop gives to each Deacon a New Testament and says,

TAKE authority to read the Gospel in the Order for Holy Communion and, and if licensed to do so, to preach the same.

Then one of the newly-ordained Deacons, appointed by the Bishop, reads the Gospel, Luke 12:35–38.

Here the Order for Holy Communion is resumed and the Deacons receive Communion with the Bishop. At the end of the Order for Holy Communion, and immediately before the Blessing, the following Collects are said.

The Making of Deacons

ALMIGHTY God, giver of all good things, you who of your great goodness have been pleased to place these your servants in the office of Deacon in your Church: Make them, we sincerely pray, to be modest, humble and faithful in their ministry and ready to observe all spiritual discipline. Grant that they may always have the testimony of a clear conscience, and continue stable and strong in your Son Jesus Christ, our Savior, to whom be glory and honor, now and forever. *Amen.*

GO before us, Lord, with your most gracious favor and accompany us with your continual help, so that in all our works begun, continued and ended in you, we may glorify your holy Name, and finally by your mercy obtain everlasting life; through Jesus Christ our Lord. *Amen.*

The Blessing

The Form and Manner of Ordaining of Priests

On the appointed day, the Service begins with Morning Prayer, which is followed immediately by a Sermon or Exhortation, in which the office and duty of those who are to be ordained Priests are declared, the necessity of the office of Priest in the Church of Christ explained, and how the people of God ought to regard those who are admitted to this office stated.

After the Sermon or Exhortation, a senior Minister presents to the Bishop (who is sitting in his Chair near to the holy Table) those who are candidates for ordination and who are appropriately robed for the occasion.

REVEREND Father in God, I present unto you these persons to be admitted to the Office of Priest.

The Bishop,

HAVE you made sure that these persons whom you present to us are truly suited and prepared, by their knowledge of Holy Scripture, sound doctrine and holiness of life, to exercise their ministry for the glory of God and the building up of his Church?

A senior Minister replies,

I HAVE examined them and I believe that they are suited and prepared for this office.

The Bishop addresses the congregation,

BROTHERS and Sisters in Christ, we intend, God willing, to receive today these persons into the holy office of Priesthood. After examining them we find that

The Ordination of Priests

they are both lawfully called to their Ministry and fit to enter into it. But if any of you knows a reason why any of these persons ought not to be received into this holy Ministry, come forward in the Name of God and make known that reason.

If any serious objection is alleged against a candidate, the Bishop shall postpone that person's ordination so that proper investigation can be made.

The Bishop proceeds by commending to the prayers of the congregation all those against whom no objection has been lodged. Here shall be said or sung the Litany, adding this Suffrage: **To bless these your servants to be admitted at this time to the Order of Priests, and to pour your grace upon them; that they may in due time exercise their office to the building up of your Church, and to the glory of your holy Name.** After the Litany the Service of Holy Communion begins with this Collect, followed by the Epistle and Gospel.

Almighty God, giver of all good things, you who by your Holy Spirit have appointed various orders of Ministry in your Church: Look in mercy upon these your servants now called to the Office of Priesthood; and so fill them with the truth of your teaching, and adorn them with holiness of life, that, both by word and by good example, they may faithfully serve you in this office, to the glory of your Name, and the building up of your Church; through the merits of our Savior Jesus Christ, who lives and reigns with you and the Holy Spirit, now and forever. *Amen*

The Epistle: Ephesians 4:1–7 · *The Gospel:* Matthew 9:36–38 or John 10:1–16

The Ordination of Priests

Sitting in his chair the Bishop says to those about to be ordained,

My brothers in Christ, you have heard, both earlier in your private examination and recently in the sermon and Scripture readings, of what dignity and great importance this Ministry is, to which you are called. In the Name of our Lord Jesus Christ, I urge you to keep in mind the nature of this office. You are called to be messengers, watchmen and stewards of the Lord; to teach and to warn, to feed and provide for the Lord's family; to seek for Christ's sheep scattered abroad in the evil world, so that they may be eternally saved through Christ.

Always have printed in your memory what a great treasure is committed to your charge. For the people whom you serve are the flock of Christ, which he purchased with his death, and for whom he shed his precious blood. The Church and congregation, whom you must serve, is both Christ's Bride and his Body. Thus, if the congregation itself, or any member of it, is hurt or hindered as a result of your negligence, God will surely discipline you for this sin. Bearing this in mind, remember what God has called you to be and to do. Never cease your work, care and diligence, until you have done all that you can possibly do, as is your duty, to bring all those under your pastoral care to a true knowledge of God, as well as to unity of faith and maturity in Christ, so that there is no place available amongst you for erroneous belief and immoral behavior.

Since this office is both so excellent in its nature and

The Ordination of Priests

so difficult in its exercise, you see how most carefully and studiously you ought to apply yourselves to this Ministry, so as to prove yourselves dutiful and thankful to the Lord, who has placed you in such a dignified position. Also you are to take care neither to offend nor to cause others to do so. Remember that it is only God himself who can give you the intention and ability to do these things. Therefore, you ought and you truly need to pray sincerely for his Holy Spirit. And, bearing in mind, that you cannot accomplish so important a work relating to the salvation of man, except by using teaching and exhortation taken out of the Holy Scriptures, and by living a life agreeable to the same, consider how seriously you ought to study and learn the Scriptures, and order your own life and that of your family, according to the rule of the same Scriptures. For this reason, you ought to forsake and set aside, as much as you can, all worldly cares and studies which hinder you doing your duty.

We are persuaded that you have carefully weighed and pondered these things for some time, and that you have clearly determined, by God's grace, to give yourselves wholly to this office, into which it has pleased God to call you, so that, to the extent of your ability, you will apply yourself wholly to this one thing, and draw all your concerns and studies towards the fulfillment of this ministry. We are also persuaded that you will continually pray to God the Father, by the mediation of our only Savior Jesus Christ, for the heavenly assistance of

The Ordination of Priests

the Holy Spirit; that, by daily reading and considering of the Scriptures, you will grow stronger in your ministry, and endeavor to sanctify and shape your lives and those of your families according to the rule and teaching of Christ, that you may be wholesome and godly examples and patterns for the people to follow.

And now, in order that this congregation of Christ's flock may also understand your minds and wills in these things, and in order to strengthen your resolve to do your duty before God, you are to answer clearly the questions which we, in the Name of God, and of his Church, now ask you.

Do you sincerely think that you are truly called, according to the will of the Lord Jesus Christ, and the canon law of this Church, to the order and ministry of Priesthood?

Answer. I do think so.

Are you persuaded that the Holy Scriptures contain sufficiently all doctrine that is necessary for eternal salvation through faith in Jesus Christ? And are you determined to teach the people committed to your pastoral care from those Scriptures, and to teach nothing as required or necessary for eternal salvation except that which you are persuaded can be proved from the Scriptures?

Answer. I am persuaded and will do so, by God's grace.

Will you always make every effort faithfully to provide the doctrine, the sacraments and the

The Ordination of Priests

discipline of Christ, as the Lord has commanded, and as this Church has received them, according to the commandments of God; so that you may teach the people under your pastoral care diligently to keep and observe the same?

Answer. I will do so, with the Lord's help.

WILL you be ready, with all faithful diligence, to banish and drive away all erroneous and strange doctrines contrary to God's Word? And will you use, as need shall require and occasion permit, private warning and public exhortation, both to the sick as well as to the healthy within your congregation, to accomplish this?

Answer. I will do so, with the Lord's help.

WILL you be diligent in prayers, in reading of the Holy Scriptures, and in such studies as assist in gaining a fuller knowledge of them? And will you at the same time lay aside worldly study and private pursuits?

Answer. I will do so, with the Lord's help.

WILL you strive to frame and fashion your own lives, and those of your families, according to the teaching of Christ? And will you make both yourselves and them, to the best of your ability, to be wholesome examples and patterns to the flock of Christ?

Answer. I will do so, with the Lord's help.

The Ordination of Priests

WILL you maintain and promote, as far as you are able, quietness, peace and love amongst all Christian people, and especially among those under your pastoral care?
Answer. I will do so, with the Lord's help.

WILL you reverently obey those who are set above you in the Church, your Bishop and other senior Ministers, and gladly and willingly accept their godly advice and submit to their considered judgments?
Answer. I will do so, with the Lord's help.

The Bishop stands and prays,

ALMIGHTY God, who has given you the will to do all these things, grant you strength and power to perform them; that he may complete the work that he has begun in you; through Jesus Christ our Lord. *Amen.*

During a period of silence the congregation is urged to pray for those to be ordained. Then, as all those to be ordained kneel, the Bishop may lead the singing of **Veni Creator Spiritus**. On occasion, a suitable alternative may be sung.

All continue in prayer as the Bishop says,

Let us pray.

ALMIGHTY God and heavenly Father, in your infinite love and goodness, you have given to us your only and most dearly beloved Son Jesus Christ, to be our Redeemer and the Author of everlasting life. After he had completed our redemption by his death, and had ascended into heaven, he sent into the world his Apostles, Prophets, Evangelists, Teachers, and Pastors, by whose

The Ordination of Priests

labor and ministry he gathered together a great flock in all parts of the world to proclaim the eternal praise of your holy Name. For these great benefits of your eternal goodness, and because you have graciously determined to call these your servants here present to the same office and ministry, which is appointed for the salvation of the world, we give you our most sincere thanks, and we praise and worship you.

And we humbly pray that through the same your Son, you will grant to all, who both here and in other places, call upon your holy Name, the readiness to show ourselves continually thankful to you for these and all your blessings; and that by the Holy Spirit we may increase daily in the knowing and believing in you and in your Son. Further, we humbly pray that by these your Ministers, and by those over whom they shall be appointed as pastors, your holy Name will be forever glorified, and your blessed kingdom enlarged; through the same your Son Jesus Christ our Lord, who lives and reigns with you in the unity of the same Holy Spirit, now and forever. *Amen.*

The Bishop, with the Priests appointed, lay their hands upon the head of each of the candidates, as in turn they kneel before the Bishop, who says,

RECEIVE the Holy Spirit for the office and work of a Priest in the Church of God, now committed to you by the laying on of our hands. Whoever's sins you forgive, they are forgiven; and whoever's sins you retain, they are retained. And be faithful in the teaching of the

The Ordination of Priests

Word of God and in the administration of his holy Sacraments, in the Name of the Father, and of the Son and of the Holy Spirit. *Amen.*

Then the Bishop gives to each a Bible, saying to him,

TAKE authority to preach the Word of God, and to administer the holy Sacraments in the congregation to which you are lawfully appointed.

When the ordinations are completed, the Nicene Creed is said or sung, and the Order for Holy Communion continues. Those who have been ordained receive Communion first and together.

After the last Collect and before the final Blessing, these two Collects are said.

MOST merciful Father, we humbly pray you to send upon these your servants your heavenly blessing, that they may be clothed with righteousness, and that your Word spoken by their mouths may have such success, that it may never be spoken in vain. Grant also that we may have grace to hear and receive what they shall proclaim and teach from your most holy Word as the means of our salvation; and grant that in all our words and deeds we may seek your glory, and the increase of your kingdom; through Jesus Christ our Lord. *Amen.*

GO before us, Lord, with your most gracious favor and accompany us with your continual help, so that in all our works begun, continued and ended in you, we may glorify your holy Name, and finally by your mercy obtain everlasting life; through Jesus Christ our Lord. *Amen.*

The Ordination of Priests

The Blessing

If on the one day some are to be made Deacons and others Priests, those to be Deacons are to be presented first, and then those to be Priests. The Litany is said or sung once but both the Collect for Deacons and that for Priests are used. The Epistle is Ephesians 4:7–13 and immediately after the Epistle are the examination and ordination of the Deacons. Then, after one of the new Deacons has read the Gospel (Matthew 9:36–38; or Luke 12:35–39) those to be ordained Priest are examined and ordained.

The Form of Ordaining or Consecrating of a Bishop

This Form is always to be used on some Sunday or Holy Day, unless for good reasons some other day is appointed.

After Morning Prayer is ended, the Archbishop (or some other Bishop duly appointed) begins the Communion Service with this Collect followed by the Epistle and Gospel, both to be read by Bishops.

ALMIGHTY God, you who by your Son Jesus Christ gave to your holy Apostles many excellent gifts, and commanded them to feed your flock: Give grace, we sincerely pray, to all Bishops, the Pastors of your Church, that they may diligently preach your Word, and duly administer its godly discipline; and grant that your people may obediently follow the same, that all may receive the crown of everlasting glory; through Jesus Christ our Lord. *Amen.*
The Epistle: Either 1 Timothy 3:1–7, or Acts 20:17–35

A psalm, hymn or spiritual song may be sung.
The Gospel: John 21:15–17, or John 20:19–23 or Matthew 28:18–20

Then is said or sung the Nicene Creed, followed by the Sermon, but on occasion this order may be reversed. Afterwards the Bishop-elect is presented by two other bishops to the Archbishop of the province.

MOST reverend Father in God, we present to you this godly and learned man to be ordained and consecrated Bishop.

The Consecration of Bishops

The testimonials of the election may be read and then the Bishop-elect takes the Oath of Obedience to the Archbishop in these words,

IN the Name of God. Amen. I *N*. elected/chosen Bishop of the Church and of the Province of *N*. (and Diocese of *N*.), do profess and promise to hold and maintain the Doctrine, Sacraments and Discipline of Christ, as the Lord has commanded in his Holy Word, and as this Church/Province has received and set forth the same; and I also promise due reverence and canonical obedience to the Archbishop of *N*. and to his successors: So help me God, through Jesus Christ.

The Archbishop calls the congregation to prayer,

BROTHERS and sisters in Christ, it is written in the Gospel of Luke that our Savior spent a whole night in prayer before he chose and sent out his twelve Apostles. It is written also in the Acts of the Apostles that the disciples at Antioch fasted and prayed before they laid hands on Paul and Barnabas, and sent them out. Let us, therefore, follow the example of Christ and his Apostles, and pray first before we admit and send out this person presented to us into the work to which we believe the Holy Spirit has called him.

Then is said or sung the Litany, with this Suffrage added, **That it may please you to bless this our Brother, Bishop-elect *N*., and to send your grace upon him, that he may duly fulfill the office into which he is called, to the building up of your Church, and to the honor, praise and glory of your Name.** Then, after the Litany is ended, this prayer is said,

The Consecration of Bishops

ALMIGHTY God, giver of all good things, you who by your Holy Spirit have appointed various orders of Ministers in your Church, look in mercy upon this your servant, N., now called to the work and ministry of a Bishop. So replenish him with the truth of your Word and adorn him with holiness of life, that he may faithfully serve you in this office, to the glory of your Name, and the building up and well-governing of your Church; through the merits of our Savior Jesus Christ, who lives and reigns with you and the Holy Spirit now and forever. *Amen.*

The Archbishop, sitting in his chair, addresses the Bishop-elect,

BROTHER, the Holy Scripture and the Canons of the Early Church command that we are not to be hasty in laying on of hands and admitting any person to governing in the Church of Christ, which he purchased with his precious blood. Therefore, before I admit you to this Ministry, I must examine you in certain important matters, so that the Congregation may witness the examination and know how you will conduct yourself in the Church of God.

Are you persuaded that you are truly called to this Ministry, according to the will of our Lord Jesus Christ, and the order of this Church?
Answer. I am so persuaded.

Are you persuaded that the Holy Scriptures contain sufficiently all doctrine required of necessity for eternal

The Consecration of Bishops

salvation through faith in Jesus Christ? And are you determined out of the same Holy Scriptures to instruct the people committed to your pastoral care, and to teach or maintain nothing as required or necessary for eternal salvation, except that which you are persuaded can be proved by Holy Scriptures?

Answer. I am so persuaded and determined, by God's grace.

Will you faithfully study and meditate upon the Holy Scriptures, and call upon God for true understanding of them, so that you will be able, by them, both to teach and encourage God's people by wholesome doctrine and to oppose and correct those who contradict it?
Answer. I will do so, with the Lord's help.

Are you ready, with all faithful diligence, to banish and drive away all erroneous and strange doctrine that is contrary to God's Word; and will you both in private and in public urge and call upon others to do the same?
Answer. I am ready to do so, with the Lord's help.

Will you deny and turn away from all ungodly and immoral lusts, and live daily a sober, righteous and godly life, so that by your example, the adversary may be put to shame and have nothing to say against you?
Answer. I will do so, with the Lord's help.

Will you maintain and promote to the best of your

The Consecration of Bishops

ability quietness, peace and love amongst all people, and will you both exercise discipline in your pastoral care, and also bring correction to the disorderly and disobedient within your charge, according to the teaching of God's Word and as canon law provides?

Answer. I will do so, with the Lord's help.

Will you be faithful in ordaining, authorizing, commissioning and laying hands on others?
Answer. I will, with the Lord's help.

Will you be gentle and merciful for Christ's sake to poor and needy people, and to all destitute strangers requiring help?
Answer. I will be so, with the Lord's help.

Then the Archbishop rises from his chair and says,

MAY Almighty God, our heavenly Father, who has given you the good desire to do all these things, grant to you strength and power to perform them, so that he may complete the work, which he has begun in you, through Jesus Christ our Lord. *Amen.*

Then the Bishop-elect is vested in the Episcopal habit, and, as he kneels, **Veni, Creator Spiritus,** or a suitable alternative, is sung or said, led by the Archbishop.

After **Veni, Creator Spiritus** the Archbishop says,

Lord, hear our prayer.
Answer. And let our cry come unto you.
Let us pray.

The Consecration of Bishops

ALMIGHTY God and most merciful Father, by your infinite goodness you have given to us your only and most dearly loved Son Jesus Christ, to be our Redeemer and the Author of everlasting life. After he had completed our salvation by his death, and had ascended into heaven, he poured down in abundance his gifts, making some Apostles, some Prophets, some Evangelists, some Pastors and Teachers, for the building up and bringing to maturity of his Church. Grant, we earnestly pray, to this your servant such grace that he may always be ready to propagate your Gospel, the good news of reconciliation with you; and also use the authority given to him not to destroy but to save, not to hurt but to help, so that as a wise and faithful steward in your household, he may at the last be received into everlasting joy; through Jesus Christ our Lord, who with you and the Holy Spirit lives and reigns, one God, now and forever. *Amen.*

> Then the Archbishop and appointed Bishops lay their hands upon the head of the Bishop-elect, as he kneels before them, and as the Archbishop says,

RECEIVE the Holy Spirit for the office and work of a Bishop in the Church of God, now committed to you by the laying on of our hands; In the Name of the Father, and of the Son and of the Holy Spirit. Amen. And remember to stir up the grace of God which is given to you by this laying on of hands, for God has not given you the spirit of fear, but of power, and love, and self-control.

The Consecration of Bishops

Then the Archbishop gives him a Bible, saying,

Commit yourself to reading, preaching and teaching. Think upon the contents of this Book, given to you. Be diligent in doing what this Book requires so that what you learn is evident to all through the quality of your life. Be disciplined in heart and life by the teaching of Scripture, so that you will both save yourself and those who hear you. Be a shepherd and not a wolf to the flock of Christ; feed them and do not harm them. Strengthen the weak, heal the sick, care for the broken-hearted, restore the backsliders, and seek the lost. Be so merciful that you are not lacking in care for anyone; and administer discipline in such a way that you do not forget mercy; so that when the Chief Shepherd appears you may receive the never-fading crown of glory; through Jesus Christ our Lord. *Amen.*

Now follows the Service of Holy Communion.

At the end of The Order for Holy Communion and before the final Blessing, these prayers are said.

Most merciful Father, we humbly ask you to send down upon this your servant your heavenly blessing; and so to endue him with your Holy Spirit, that, preaching your Word, he may not only be diligent to reprove, exhort and rebuke with all patience and sound teaching; but, also, he may be a wholesome example in word, in life, in love, in faith, and in purity; that faithfully fulfilling his vocation, he may at the last day receive the crown of righteousness, laid up by the Lord

The Consecration of Bishops

the righteous Judge, who lives and reigns one God with the Father and the Holy Spirit, now and forever. *Amen.*

Go before us, Lord, with your most gracious favor and accompany us with your continual help, so that in all our works begun, continued and ended in you, we may glorify your holy Name, and finally by your mercy obtain everlasting life; through Jesus Christ our Lord. *Amen.*

The Blessing

The Thirty-Nine Articles of Religion

Articles agreed upon by the Archbishops and Bishops of both Provinces [Canterbury and York] in the Convocation held at London in the year 1562 and here presented in a contemporary English form. Only the original text has the status of a Formulary of the Church. For maximum benefit, this contemporary version should be read alongside the original text.

1. Faith in The Holy Trinity

There is only one living and true God. His existence is everlasting, without beginning or end. He is a Spiritual Being, not limited by a body and bodily members, and free from bodily desires and impulses. His power, wisdom, and goodness are infinite. He is the Creator and Preserver of all things whether visible or invisible. In the unity of this one true God there are three Persons, the Father, the Son, and the Holy Spirit, who are one in being, power and eternity.

2. The Word or Son of God who was made true Man

The Son, who is the Word of the Father, is the Son of the Father from everlasting to everlasting. He is truly and eternally God, one with the Father in being. He took our human nature to himself in the womb of the Virgin Mary, so that two full and perfect natures, his divine and our human nature, were united in the one Person of the incarnate Son, never to be divided. There is, therefore, one Christ, who is truly God and truly

The Articles of Religion

man, and who truly suffered, was crucified, died and was buried. By Christ's sacrifice of himself, not only for original guilt but also for all actual sins of men, God was reconciling the world to himself (2 Corinthians 5:19).

3. Christ's descent into Hell

As Christ died for us and was buried, so also it is to be believed that he descended into hell.

4. The Resurrection of Christ

Christ truly rose again from the dead. His was a bodily resurrection, with flesh, bones and all things that belong to the perfection of our human nature. Further, his ascension was a bodily ascension into heaven, where he is now enthroned at the Father's right hand until the last day, when he will return to judge all men.

5. The Holy Spirit

The Holy Spirit who proceeds from the Father and the Son is one in being, majesty and glory with the Father and the Son, and thus is truly and eternally God.

6. The sufficiency of Holy Scripture for salvation

Holy Scripture contains everything that is necessary for our salvation. Consequently, nobody should be required to believe as an article of the Christian faith, or to regard as necessary for salvation, anything that is not found in Scripture or that cannot be proved from Scripture. By the term Holy Scripture we mean the canonical books of the Old and New Testaments, namely:

The Articles of Religion

Genesis, Exodus, Leviticus, Numbers, Deuteronomy, Joshua, Judges, Ruth, 1 and 2 Samuel, 1 and 2 Kings, 1 and 2 Chronicles, Ezra, Nehemiah, Esther, Job, Psalms, Proverbs, Ecclesiastes, Song of Songs, Isaiah, Jeremiah, Lamentations, Ezekiel, Daniel, Hosea, Joel, Amos, Obadiah, Jonah, Micah, Nahum, Habakkuk, Zephaniah, Haggai, Zechariah, Malachi. And also, Matthew, Mark, Luke, John, Acts, Romans, 1 and 2 Corinthians, Galatians, Ephesians, Philippians, Colossians, 1 and 2 Thessalonians, 1 and 2 Timothy, Titus, Philemon, Hebrews, James, 1 and 2 Peter, 1, 2 and 3 John, Jude, Revelation.

The books known as the Apocrypha or as Deutero-Canonical are read by the Church, as Jerome said, because of the examples they provide of heroic lives and faithful conduct; but the Church does not use these books to establish any doctrine. These are their titles: The First Book of Esdras, The Second Book of Esdras, Tobit, Judith, The Rest of Esther, The Wisdom of Solomon, Ecclesiasticus or the Wisdom of Jesus son of Sirach, Baruch, A Letter of Jeremiah, The Song of the Three, Daniel and Susanna, Daniel, Bel and the Snake, The Prayer of Manasseh, The First Book of Maccabees, and The Second Book of Maccabees.

7. The Old Testament

The Old Testament is not contrary to the New Testament. In the Old as well as in the New Testament, everlasting life is offered to mankind through Christ; this is because as both God and man, he is the only

Mediator between God and man. Therefore, we must not pay attention to any who say that in the Old Testament the patriarchs and other godly persons were limited in their expectation to transitory promises. Although the ceremonies and rites of the Law which God gave through Moses are not binding on Christians, and the civil precepts of the Law are not essential for the organization of any state or commonwealth, yet no Christian person at all is free from obedience to the commandments known as moral.

8. The Three Creeds

The three creeds, namely the Nicene Creed, the Athanasian Creed, and what is commonly called the Apostles' Creed, should be received and believed without reservation, because they may be proved from Holy Scripture.

9. Original sin

Original sin does not consist in imitating the sin of Adam (as the Pelagians wrongly teach), but is the fault and corruption of the nature with which all the descendants of Adam are born. It is due to original sin that we have departed very far from the original righteousness in which we were created, and are naturally inclined to evil, with the result that there is a constant war between the flesh and the spirit. Accordingly in every person born into this world, original sin is deserving of God's wrath and condemnation. This infection of our nature remains even in those who are reborn in and by Christ.

Because of original sin the desire of the flesh is not submissive to the Law of God. True though it is that there is no condemnation awaiting those who believe and are baptized, yet the Apostle asserts that all ungodly desires are in themselves sinful (Romans 6:12; 7:7).

10. Free Will

Since the fall of Adam, man's state is such that he is unable, by his own natural strength and good works, to turn and dispose himself to believe the Gospel and call upon God. Consequently, we have no power of our own to do good works that are pleasing and acceptable to God, unless the grace of God is first given to us through Christ, so that we may have a good will, and that same grace continues at work within us to maintain that good will.

11. Justification

It is not because of any good works or deservings on our part, but only by faith which rests on the merit of our Lord and Saviour Jesus Christ, that we are accounted righteous before God. Therefore the doctrine that we are justified by faith alone is most edifying and full of strength and comfort. (This doctrine is more fully explained in the Homily on Justification in the First Book of Homilies.)

12. Good Works

Although good works, which are the fruits of faith and follow after our justification, cannot put away our sins, and are subject to the severity of God's judgment, yet, since they are done in Christ and for his sake, they are pleasing and acceptable to God; for they spring necessarily from a true and vital faith, and are indeed the evidence of a vital faith, just as a tree is recognized by its fruit.

13. Works before Justification

Works that are done before receiving the grace of Christ and the indwelling of his Spirit are not pleasing to God, because they do not spring from faith in Jesus Christ; nor is it true (as some say) that they render us fit to receive grace or are deserving of grace. On the contrary, the fact that such works are not done as God has willed and commanded them to be done can only mean that they have the nature of sin.

14. Works of Supererogation

Works, which are supposedly done voluntarily beyond and in excess of what is required by God's commandments (known as works of supererogation), cannot be taught without self-centered arrogance and irreverence; for it is claimed that persons who perform such works render to God not only as much as it is their duty to render, but actually do for God more than is of binding duty required; whereas Christ plainly stated, "When you have done all that is commanded, say, We are unprofitable servants" (Luke 17:10).

15. Christ alone without sin

As our true fellow man, Christ was like us in all respects, with the exception only of sin, from which he was completely free, both in his flesh and in his spirit. He came into the world to be the Lamb without spot or blemish, and by his once-for-all sacrifice of himself to take away the sins of the world as the one in whom, as St John says, there was no sin (John 1:29, 1 John 3:5). But all the rest of us, even though we have been baptized and born again in Christ, continue to offend in many things; and "if we say we have no sin we deceive ourselves and the truth is not in us" (1 John 1:8).

16. Sin after Baptism

Not every serious sin committed after our baptism is an unpardonable sin against the Holy Spirit. So persons, who fall into sin after baptism, should be encouraged to repent. After we have received the Holy Spirit, it is possible for us to turn away from the grace we have experienced and to fall into sin, and it is possible for us, who have fallen, to rise again and amend our lives by the grace of God. Therefore, persons, who say that they cannot sin any more as long as they continue in this life (claiming to have attained sinless perfection), or who deny any opportunity of forgiveness to those who truly repent, are to be condemned.

17. Predestination and election

Predestination to life belongs to God's everlasting purpose. By this is meant that before the foundation of the world, it is his unchangeable decree, in accordance with his secret counsel, to deliver from the curse and damnation those whom he has chosen in Christ, and

The Articles of Religion

to bring them by him to everlasting salvation, as vessels of his mercy (Romans 9:21ff). So, those on whom such an excellent blessing of God is bestowed are called according to God's purpose by the Holy Spirit working in them in God's good time; through grace they obey this calling and are freely justified by God; they become the sons of God by adoption (Romans 3:24; 8:15f.); they are conformed to the image of his only Son Jesus Christ; they lead holy lives that are given to good works to the glory of God; and at last, by God's mercy, they attain to everlasting bliss (Romans 8:29f; Ephesians 2:8–10).

The reverent consideration of our predestination and election in Christ is full of sweet, pleasant and unspeakable strength and comfort to godly persons, who feel the working in themselves of the Spirit of Christ, mortifying the works of the flesh and their earthly passions and drawing their thoughts upward to high and heavenly realities. This teaching is welcome to us both because it strongly establishes and confirms our assurance of eternal salvation to be enjoyed through Christ, and also because it kindles in us a fervent love to God. For unregenerate persons, however, who are moved by idle curiosity and who do not have the Spirit of Christ, to be constantly confronted with the doctrine of God's predestination is dangerous and disastrous, since the devil uses it to drive them either to despair or to abandon themselves to immoral and ungodly living, which is no less perilous than despair.

Furthermore, we must accept God's promises in

the way in which they are ordinarily presented to us in Holy Scripture, and in all that we do the will of God is to be followed precisely as it is revealed to us in the Word of God.

18. Salvation in Christ alone

They are to be condemned as false teachers who assert that persons will be saved no matter what beliefs they hold or what sect they belong to, provided they sincerely lead their lives according to those beliefs and to the light of nature; for Holy Scripture insists that it is only by the Name of Jesus Christ that we may be saved (Acts 4:12).

19. The Church

The visible Church of Christ is an assembly of believing people in which the pure Word of God is preached and the Sacraments are ministered with due order and discipline as ordained by Christ. Together with other Churches (e.g. of Jerusalem, Alexandria and Antioch), the Church of Rome has erred, not only in matters of conduct and ceremonial but also in matters of doctrine.

20. The Authority of the Church

The Church has power to prescribe rites and ceremonies and has authority in theological controversies; but it is not lawful for the Church to prescribe anything that is contrary to God's written Word, or to expound one passage of Scripture in such a way that it disagrees with another. Therefore, although the Church is a witness

The Articles of Religion

and a guardian of Holy Scripture, yet it is not open to it to prescribe anything contrary to Scripture, or to enforce anything not found in Scripture to be believed as necessary to salvation.

21. The Authority of General Councils

General Councils may not be called without the authority of Christian Rulers. When they meet they may err, and sometimes have erred, even in issues of theological importance (for such Councils are composed of men, not all of whom may be governed by the Spirit and the Word of God). So nothing declared by such Councils as necessary for salvation has binding power or authority unless it is plainly taught in Holy Scripture.

22. Purgatory

The Romish teaching about purgatory, pardons, the worship and adoration of images and relics, and also the practice of praying to saints, is a futile deception, which, far from being grounded in Scripture, is repugnant to the Word of God.

23. Ministering in the Congregation

No man is permitted to take upon himself the office of public preaching or ministration of the Sacraments before he has been called and appointed to fulfill this office. And those persons should be accepted as lawfully called and appointed, who have been selected and called to this work by men entrusted with public authority in the Church to call and send ministers into the Lord's vineyard.

24. The Language of Public Worship

It is plainly incompatible with the Word of God and with the custom of the primitive Church to conduct public worship, or to minister the Sacraments in the Church, in a language the people do not understand.

25. The Sacraments

The Sacraments prescribed by Christ are badges and tokens of our profession as Christians, and, more particularly, they are trustworthy witnesses and effectual signs of God's grace and good will to us. By them God works invisibly in us, both arousing and also strengthening and confirming our faith in him.

Christ our Lord has ordained two gospel Sacraments, namely Baptism and the Lord's Supper.

The five that are commonly called sacraments, namely, confirmation, penance, ordination, matrimony, and extreme unction are not to be received as sacraments of the gospel, since they have in part developed from a false understanding of apostolic practice and in part represent states of life allowed in the Scriptures. Moreover, because they have no visible sign or ceremony commanded by God, they do not belong in the same category as the Sacraments of Baptism and the Lord's Supper. The Sacraments were not appointed by Christ to be a public spectacle or to be paraded for adoration, but to be used with due discipline. They have a beneficial effect and work only in those who receive them worthily; whereas those who receive them unworthily bring condemnation on themselves, as St Paul teaches (1 Corinthians 11:27ff).

26. The Unworthiness of Ministers

In the visible Church there is always a mingling of evil with good, and at times evil persons hold the chief positions in the ministry of the Word and Sacraments. Yet, because they do so, not in their own but in Christ's name, and perform their ministry by his commission and authority, we may avail ourselves of their ministry both in hearing the Word of God and in receiving the Sacraments. The effect of Christ's ordinance is not taken away by their wickedness, nor is the grace of God's gifts diminished in the case of those who receive the Sacraments rightly and by faith; for, although ministered by evil men, these are effectual on account of Christ's institution and promise.

Nevertheless, it belongs to the discipline of the Church that evil ministers should be investigated and that they should be accused by those who have knowledge of their offences, and, further, that, on being found guilty, they should by just judgment be deposed.

27. Baptism

Baptism is a sign of the faith we profess and a mark that differentiates Christian persons from those who are not united to Christ; and it is also a sign of regeneration or new birth by which, as by an instrument, those who receive baptism rightly are grafted into the Church, the promises of forgiveness of sin and of our adoption to be the sons of God are visibly signified and sealed, and faith is confirmed and grace increased by virtue of prayer to God. The baptism of young children is under all circumstances to be retained in the Church as a practice fully agreeable with the institution of Christ.

28. The Lord's Supper

The Supper of the Lord is not only a sign of the love that Christians ought to have among themselves for each other, but is especially a Sacrament of our redemption by Christ's death. Accordingly, for those who rightly, worthily, and with faith receive it the bread that is broken is a partaking of the body of Christ and the cup of blessing is a partaking of the blood of Christ (1 Corinthians 10:16).

Transubstantiation (the teaching that the substance of the bread and wine is changed into the actual flesh and blood of Christ) in the Supper of the Lord cannot be proved by Holy Scripture, but is repugnant to the plain words of Scripture, overthrows the nature of a sacrament, and has given rise to many superstitions.

In the Lord's Supper the body of Christ is given, taken and eaten only in a heavenly or spiritual manner, and faith is the means by which the body of Christ is received and eaten in the Supper.

The sacrament of the Lord's Supper was not commanded by Christ to be reserved, carried about, lifted up or worshipped.

29. The Lord's Supper and Participation by the Unrepentant

Though wicked persons, and all in whom a vital faith is absent, physically and visibly press the Sacrament of the body and blood of Christ with their teeth (as Saint Augustine says), yet in no sense are they partakers of Christ; on the contrary, they eat and drink the sign or Sacrament of so great a heavenly reality to their own condemnation.

30. Communion in Two Kinds

The cup of the Lord is not to be denied to the laity, for both parts of the Lord's Sacrament, the wine as well as the bread, ought by Christ's ordinance and commandment to be ministered alike to all Christian persons.

31. The One Offering of Christ

Christ's offering of himself on the cross, once for all, is the perfect redemption, propitiation, and satisfaction for all the sins of the whole world, both original and actual, and there is no other satisfaction for sin, but that alone. So the sacrifices of masses, in which it is commonly said that the priest offers Christ for the living and the dead, to obtain the remission of their punishment or guilt, are blasphemous fables and dangerous deceits.

32. The Marriage of Priests

Bishops, priests and deacons are not commanded by God's law to take vows of celibacy or to abstain from marriage; therefore it is lawful for them, as for all other Christian persons, to marry at their own discretion, where they judge that it serves better to godliness for them to do so.

33. Excommunicated Persons

Any person, who by open discipline of the Church is rightly cut off from the unity of the Church and excommunicated, ought to be treated by the whole company of the faithful as a heathen and a traitor, until such time as he is reconciled by penitence and received back into the Church by a judge with authority to do so (cf., Matthew 18:17).

34. The Traditions of the Church

It is not necessary that traditions and ceremonies should be uniform and identical in every place; for these have at all times been varied, and they may be changed to accord with the diversities of countries, times, and human customs, provided that nothing be ordained contrary to God's Word. Anyone, who by his private judgment willingly and deliberately breaks the traditions and ceremonies of the Church (which are not repugnant to the Word of God, and are appointed and approved by common authority), ought to be openly rebuked. This is in order that others may fear to follow his example, as one who offends against the common order of the Church, undermines authority, and wounds the consciences of weak fellow Christians.

Every particular or national church has authority to prescribe, change and abolish ceremonies or rites of the Church which have been ordered only by human authority, providing all things are done for edification.

35. The Homilies

The two books of Homilies, which were set forth in the times of Edward VI and Elizabeth I respectively, contain godly and wholesome teaching, and ought carefully to be read.

36. The Consecration of Bishops and other Ministers

The form of consecration of Archbishops and Bishops and the ordering of Priests and Deacons, set forth in the time of Edward VI, contain all things necessary for such consecration and ordering and nothing that of itself is superstitious and ungodly. Therefore, anyone who is consecrated or ordained according to these rites we declare to be rightly, orderly and lawfully consecrated and ordained.

37. Civil Magistrates

We do not give to our princes or rulers the right to minister either God's Word or the Sacraments. The only prerogative, which we recognize as having been given by God himself in Holy Scripture to all godly rulers, is that they should rule all states and classes committed to their charge by God, whether ecclesiastical or secular, and restrain with the civil sword stubborn persons and evildoers.

The Bishop of Rome has no jurisdiction in this realm.

Christians may be punished by the laws of the realm with death for heinous and grievous offences.

It is lawful for Christian men to carry weapons and serve in wars at the command of the civil ruler.

38. Private Property

The wealth and possessions of Christians are not common to all, nor is their right and title to own private property to be questioned. Nevertheless, every person ought to give liberally and according to his ability from the things he possesses to the poor.

39. Oath-taking

While we acknowledge that vain and rash swearing is forbidden to Christians by our Lord Jesus Christ and by St. James (Matthew 5:34–37; James 5:12), we judge that our Christian religion does not prohibit us from swearing an oath, when it is required by the magistrate in the cause of good faith and charity, providing it is done according to the Prophet's teaching in justice, judgment and truth.

Acknowledgements

The three editions of *The Book of Common Prayer* (1662, 1928, 1962), in the traditional English language of Prayer and Public Worship, have provided the solid basis from which this contemporary English rendering of services in the tradition of Anglican Common Prayer has been created.

The statement concerning "The Christian Year" is based upon that provided in *The Shorter Prayer Book* (London 1946) of the Church of England.

Most of the verses of Scripture used are taken from the English Standard Version (copyright, Crossway Bibles of Good News Publishers, 2001) or from The Revised Version (copyright 1971, 1973 by the Division of Christian Education of the National Council of the Churches of Christ in the U.S.A.). Either or both of these translations are recommended for use with the Liturgy in this book.

Various general possibilities for a contemporary form of the Common Prayer tradition were learned from both *An English Prayer Book* (Church Society and Oxford University Press, 1994) and *Common Worship* (Church House Publishing, London, 2000).

The translation of the Office Hymn, *Phos Hilaron*, is based on that provided in *Common Worship*.

The translation of the short Office Hymn for Compline is provided by the Communities' Consultative Council, Norwich, England.

The English form of The Athanasian Creed is adapted from the Latin and English texts provided by J.N.D. Kelly in *The Athanasian Creed* (London, 1964), and by the Church Society in *An English Prayer Book*.

The expression, "psalms, hymns and spiritual songs," used in rubrics is from Ephesians 5:19.

The Two Books of Homilies which are described in Article 35 are published by Edgeways Books in Great Britain—www.edgewaysbooks.com